# LEAPFROGGING INEQUALITY

*Remaking*

# LEAPFROGGING

*Education to Help*

# INEQUALITY

*Young People Thrive*

REBECCA WINTHROP

*with* ADAM BARTON *and* EILEEN McGIVNEY

BROOKINGS INSTITUTION PRESS

*Washington, D.C.*

Skills for a Changing World is a project of the Center for Universal Education at Brookings that seeks to ensure all children have high-quality learning opportunities, which build the breadth of skills needed to create vibrant, healthy societies in the face of changing social, technological, and economic demands.

*Library of Congress Cataloging-in-Publication data are available.*

ISBN 978-0-8157-3570-0 (pbk. : alk. paper)
ISBN 978-0-8157-3571-7 (epub)

9 8 7 6 5 4 3 2 1

Typeset in Adobe Garamond Pro

Composition by Elliott Beard

# Contents

# Figures and Tables

# Acknowledgments

This book is based on the Center for Universal Education's report *Can We Leapfrog? The Potential of Education Innovations to Rapidly Accelerate Progress*, first published in September 2017 by Rebecca Winthrop and Eileen McGivney with Adam Barton. We are indebted to many people who provided valuable insights first during the research process and then during the writing of the report and the book. First and foremost, we are grateful to Priya Shankar and Timothy P. Williams, who provided crucial assistance with our research. We also thank our exceptional interns—Bogdan Bors, Mackenzie Fusco, Bhavani Khemka, Elena Losada, and Alexander Wheeler—for their support and commitment. We also thank our colleagues and friends, who gave feedback and comments, as well as the many innovators and thinkers whose experiences shaped the research project through interviews. We are particularly grateful to Esther Care, Luis Crouch, David Baker, Marcela Escobari, Justin van Fleet, Julia Gillard, David Istance, Helyn Kim, John Moravec, and Jenny Perlman Robinson for their invaluable feedback and comments.

The Brookings Institution is a nonprofit organization devoted to independent research and policy solutions. Its mission is to conduct high-quality independent research and, based on that research, to provide innovative, practical recommendations for policymakers and the public.

Acknowledgments

The conclusions and recommendations of any Brookings publication are solely those of its author(s) and do not reflect the views of the Institution, its management, or its other scholars.

Brookings gratefully acknowledges the program support provided to the Center for Universal Education by the Government of Norway, the LEGO Foundation, and the William and Flora Hewlett Foundation.

Brookings recognizes that the value it provides is in its absolute commitment to quality, independence, and impact. Activities supported by its donors reflect this commitment.

## One

# Introduction: Inequality Driven by Education

The deep inequalities between the rich and the poor are increasingly of concern to citizens around the world and have been hotly debated by politicians and policy analysts. Public debates on inequality cross national borders and traditional political lines. Citizen engagement and protests span from the global Occupy Wall Street movement to the recent international populist backlash against globalization and immigration. Economists at the International Monetary Fund, who are best known for their work in securing global financial security, have called widening income inequality "the defining challenge of our time," arguing that such inequality puts economic growth at risk.[1]

Inequality is at some of its highest levels in decades within wealthy countries, and it remains a pernicious challenge in poorer ones. The drivers of inequality, from tax policy to financial exclusion, are often discussed in policy circles. However, one important but less frequently debated reason for inequality is education. Over the course of the twentieth century, as mass schooling spread virtually throughout the world, an individual's level of educational attainment became one of the most important factors determining his or her income and status in society. Sociologists of education have traced how different social mechanisms for achieving wealth and status in society, from marriage to family to guilds to religion to occupation, may have retained some of their traditional force in certain parts of the world but today largely have given way to schooling as the primary currency for social advancement.[2]

The United States provides a good illustration of this phenomenon. Richard Reeves, in his latest research on social mobility in America, shows that parents' educational level is even more influential than their income level on their children's eventual position on the economic ladder, especially when looking at parents in the top 20 percent of education and income levels. Of course, in the United States, parents with more money are more likely to be able to move into areas with good schools, and so parents' ability to give their children a good education is connected with their available financial resources. The United States ultimately is a country where "the children and grandchildren of wealthy people end up wealthy themselves, but largely by getting a better education than through direct inheritance: because of B.A.s rather than bequests."[3]

As a result, for the United States and for many other countries across Latin America, Europe, Africa, and Asia, efforts to address inequality must include finding ways to give all young people a good-quality education. The effort to speed up the pace of change in education, or "leapfrog" educational progress, is critical at this moment in time. Luckily, in many corners of the globe, including across the United States, educators are working tirelessly on approaches that may help education do just that.

## Leapfrogging Inequality: A Case Study from India

Surrounded by rice fields, the small rural village of Bhaumau in Uttar Pradesh—India's most populous state—is tapping into new people and places to help educate its children for the twenty-first century. Most children in the village have enrolled in local schools and, with help from the nonprofit organization Pratham, are mastering basic reading and numeracy. But outside school in the late afternoons, children are complementing their school-based learning by honing a wide range of skills through a combination of play, peer learning, technology, and light-touch parental oversight.

Groups of five or six children between ages 8 and 14 huddle together with offline tablet computers, which are loaded with educational content in Hindi and English and updated manually every few months by Pratham field staff. The tablets help the children develop their skills, from digital literacy to critical thinking to teamwork, and they not only consume content but also make content by filming short skits and interviewing visitors. They constantly experiment with new projects, and in the process they practice and apply language, math, and science knowledge. The main role of their parents is to ensure that the tablets are charged in the evening, using either the sporadic electricity provided by the government or generator power.

Since the children of Bhaumau have been playing with the tablets, their assessment scores on academic subjects have increased markedly, especially in English. Perhaps more important, they are developing powerful learning-to-learn skills that will help them innovate, create, and thrive in a fast-changing world. Indeed, within the first three months of the program, these children, who had rarely encountered technology more complicated than a mobile phone, outsmarted the Pratham field staff by hacking most of the tablets' passwords, which enabled the children to add their own content to the tablets' existing repository.[4]

The village's schools rarely use this type of student-centered learning; the average teacher relies on more traditional, instruction-based approaches. Even when schools have special programs to incorporate technology, this does not necessarily translate into student-centered learning experiences. For instance, in one of Bhaumau's nearby villages, an extra classroom has been added to an elementary school and equipped with desktop computers. Yet students spend their class time there following the instructor's directions about how to use a software package, including filling in questions in an accompanying workbook describing the layout of the keyboard and the purpose of computers. In contrast, the students testing the limits of the tablets in Bhaumau are having the kinds of playful, dynamic learning experiences needed if they are to master not only essential academic skills such as literacy and numeracy, but also broader and equally crucial skills such as critical thinking, collaboration, empathy, communication, and problem solving. If the children in the modest village of Bhaumau, where most parents are day laborers and agriculture workers, can experience such a rich learning environment with dramatic early results in a few short months, rather than the years or decades typical of education reform, why should this not happen elsewhere?

The Bhaumau children's experiences epitomize the underlying motivation for this report: to explore the possibility of harnessing innovations to leapfrog—to jump ahead, or move rapidly and nonlinearly—to make educational progress. We are less interested in the leapfrogging potential of one particular innovation over another, and we are agnostic about which sorts of actors drive these innovations. They may be governments, as is the case with the Indian government's recent move to set up "tinkering labs" in public schools. They may include civil society organizations, as in the case of the students in Bhaumau. They may also involve the private sector, as with the Indian adaptive learning product called Mindspark, which effectively supports students' in-class learning. Instead, we are most interested in exploring globally what leapfrogging in education looks like—and the potential for education innovations to help us leap ahead.

Our aim in this book is to share insights that can inspire action-oriented governments, civil society organizations, educators, philanthropic investors, and members of the business community to seriously consider the prospect of rapid, nonlinear educational progress and to reflect on what more needs to be done to make leapfrogging in education a reality. Ultimately, we hope that these education actors adopt a leapfrog mind-set when advancing their work.

## Why Do We Need to Leapfrog?

The book's second chapter lays out the case for leapfrogging. It presents two main global education challenges: skills inequality and skills uncertainty. First, in most countries around the world, schools serve some children well and some poorly. This inequality in how formal education systems develop children's skills and abilities is found both within countries, between wealthy and poor children, and among countries, between the developed world's high-income countries and the developing world's low-income countries. What is more worrisome is that, with the current pace of change, it will take decades and centuries—a veritable "100-year gap"—for poor children to catch up with the educational levels of to-day's wealthy children. Second, this 100-year gap becomes more daunting when it is viewed as the difference between what we consider to be good or bad education today, an assessment that does not take into account the type of education that children will need for the future. Fast-paced social and economic change means that it is not clear exactly what skills children will need to thrive in the future world of work and to be constructive citizens. Nonetheless, children will need to be well equipped to face uncertainty, and to, among other things, work collaboratively with others to solve problems—a skill seldom taught in the average school.

## What Is Leapfrogging?

The third chapter defines leapfrogging, a concept not usually applied to education. It argues that the average schooling model used in most countries—what we call the persistent Prussian model, given its origins in mid-1700s Prussia—has brought many social and economic benefits to society. Thus, we should think carefully about what needs to be transformed to meet the twin challenges of skills inequality and skills uncertainty. Two of the most important transformations needed are in what children learn—that is, schooling must focus on a breadth of skills (box 1-1), including but going beyond academics—and how children learn, that is, schooling must put students' curiosity at the center of the teaching and learning process and make room for hands-on, playful, and experiential learning. Given these goals, we define leapfrogging as any practices, both new and old, that can address skills inequality and skills uncertainty at the same time, and much more quickly than the current 100-year gap predicts. Leapfrogging should set its sights on helping all children develop a breadth of skills, regardless of whether they are currently in or out of school or are living in poor or rich communities. Ultimately, we hope that educator actors adopt a leapfrog mind-set, one that breaks from the well-established logic of prioritizing, first, access to school; second, academic quality; and third, real-world relevance. Indeed, in most countries, mass education has developed following this stepwise approach: expanding schooling access over time; then, once children are in school, working to improve the quality of core academic subjects; and finally focusing on cultivating the skills needed to thrive in the world.

Finally, although leapfrogging often connotes ideas of skipping over steps to advance along a particular path, we do not stick narrowly to this idea. We took inspiration from the overarching concept that rapid and nonlinear progress can be made without following the usual path, perhaps skipping steps but also possibly ending up in a new place altogether.

## What Can Be Done to Leapfrog?

The fourth chapter introduces the role of innovation in helping education to leapfrog. One of the major questions the global education community faces—the education paradox of our time—is whether it is possible to simultaneously address both skills inequality and skills uncertainty. This paradox acknowledges that the current ways we help schools better teach the most marginalized, and in doing so address skills inequality, often reinforce the formal education structures that prevent students from developing the breadth of skills they need for 21st-century life and therefore do not prepare them for skills uncertainty. Citing the International Commission on Financing Global Education Opportunity, we argue that education innovation has a role to play in finding ways to leapfrog. Ultimately, innovation—an idea or technology that is a break from previous practice, and is often new in a particular context, even if not new to the world—can help countries that want to prepare all children for a fast-changing world but are "hitting the limits" of what their education systems can provide.[5]

## In What Ways Can We Leapfrog?

The fifth chapter presents our two major contributions to the effort to explore how education can leapfrog: a leapfrog pathway based on existing evidence about how to transform what and how children learn; and a global catalog of education innovations that suggest ways to help ed-

---

**BOX 1-1**  Breadth of Skills

"Breadth of skills" refers to the expanded set of skills that education systems should help young people develop. Traditional skills, such as literacy and numeracy, must be complemented with skills such as collaboration, problem solving, and creativity. Children's cognitive, social, and emotional abilities must be brought to bear in developing their breadth of skills. "Breadth of skills" is used in this book interchangeably with terms such as "broad range of skills," "diverse skill set," or "21st-century skills."

---

ucation hop, skip, or leap to different destinations along this pathway. The pathway charts a vision for leapfrogging that recognizes context and leaves room for ongoing growth. Depending on the starting conditions of education, progress can include a hop, a skip, or a full leap toward enabling all children and youth to develop the broad set of skills they need. A "hop" includes approaches found at the start of our pathway; they can address skills inequality even if they do not address skills uncertainty—an important point of progress for marginalized children. A "skip" involves approaches in the middle of the pathway; they lay the groundwork for addressing skills inequality and skills uncertainty at the same time. Finally, a true "leap" addresses both skills inequality and uncertainty; it can occur only when the core elements of innovations are aligned at the end of the pathway. The pathway provides a map for education actors, on which they can place their own work and against which they can assess it. But what evidence is there that leapfrogging is possible in the here and now? We chose to scan the landscape of education innovations and develop the catalog based on our interest in grounding the theory about leapfrogging in existing practice. We wanted to learn what is realistically possible today and in the near future and how education innovations stack up against the pathway.

To develop the catalog, we compiled the lists of 16 organizations that we call Education Innovation Spotters. These organizations currently are examining different innovative programs, schools, policies, approaches, and tools; collecting information about them; highlighting them in publicly accessible formats; and sometimes funding or supporting them. This catalog consists of almost 3,000 education innovations analyzed in relation to the four main elements of our leapfrog pathway, and this chapter gives illustrative examples from the catalog that showcase these elements in practice.

## Where Is the Potential to Leapfrog?

This sixth chapter reflects on the current state of the education innovations community—the many actors worldwide who are engaged in supporting innovative education practices—and its collective potential to help education leapfrog. In many ways, the education innovations community is well positioned to advance leapfrogging; more than 85 percent of countries host innovations included in our catalog, which focuses heavily on poor and marginalized children. The vast majority of innovations center on efforts to change the teaching and learning process by using more playful learning approaches, and different actors have found ways to cooperate with government, civil society groups, and the private sector to implement their new approaches. However, there are also noticeable gaps that could limit the ability of the education innovations to help fuel leapfrogging. For example, few efforts prioritize teachers' professional development as a main aim of innovation, a factor that is essential for leaping ahead. Other comparatively neglected factors include finding new ways to recognize learning, to use technology to transform education, and to make effectiveness data publicly available. There are also significant gaps in the types of innovations that Innovation Spotters highlight: relatively few of these selected innovations are government-led, intended for children living in crisis and conflict, or focused on children with disabilities. Undoubtedly, many actors around the world are pursuing innovative education approaches in these areas; an effort to highlight such innovations would greatly enrich the community's knowledge.

Ultimately, we conclude that governments, funders, and practitioners—and all those interested in helping leapfrog education to give young people the full range of skills they will need to thrive—should be optimistic about the potential to rapidly accelerate progress. The education innovations community is energetic, diverse, and widespread, and it appears to be willing to experiment with the persistent Prussian model of schooling. In many corners of the globe, the leapfrog mind-set is alive and well. Children from poor and wealthy families alike are participating in new approaches that have shown impressive results in changing how schooling is delivered, what is taught, and how teaching is done. This richness of education innovations holds promise for leapfrogging—addressing skills inequality and skills uncertainty—especially if the education innovations community can do a better job of mitigating current gaps and governments can provide a conducive environment for effective innovations to thrive and be scaled up.

## *Two*

# Why Do We Need to Leapfrog?

### The Persistent Prussian Model

It was not until 1763 that the idea of mass schooling began to take root. Prussia, following the protracted conflict of the Seven Years' War that had engulfed much of Europe in the mid-1700s, sought innovative ideas to strengthen its position in the world—specifically, the general capability of its men in uniform. Its solution was to establish the world's first system of compulsory and universal education.[1] A century later, this idea caught on in the United States, when education reformer Horace Mann led the Common Schools movement in Massachusetts.[2] Mass schooling began to spread across Asia and Latin America, and at the end of the 20th century, especially after the 1989 United Nations Convention on the Rights of the Child, countries across Africa began to push for universal schooling.[3]

This spread of mass schooling around the globe is, in the words of the education sociologist David Baker, an "education revolution."[4] For most of human history, it was virtually unimaginable that, within four generations, schooling would become a central feature of children's lives worldwide. Indeed, in the past 200 years, the number of children enrolled in primary schooling globally soared from 2.3 million at the beginning of the 19th century to more than 700 million today, over 40 times the rate of population growth.[5]

Democratic and authoritarian countries alike shared this rapid growth in the idea and practice of mass schooling. The rise of the university in Europe, some 900 years ago, brought with it a radical belief for the time: that knowledge and truth are open to discovery by anybody and that education institutions, not other social institutions such as the church, are the arbiters of this information. Schools facilitated access to this knowledge. Centuries later, as economies, particularly in the West, shifted from agriculture to manufacturing, the need for new skills also drove the social demand for mass schooling. But mass schooling was by no means of interest only to industrializing economies. The global spread of mass schooling, especially after World War II, was driven by a combination of nationalism and the idea that education is a fundamental right for all children—a concept embraced by families, activists, and aid agencies around the world.[6]

However, today's approach to schooling has plenty of critics. On December 10, 2006, *Time* magazine ran a story on education, which argued that if the fabled Rip van Winkle suddenly woke up from a century of slumber, he would be hard-pressed to recognize anything in the world around him—except a school. Though he would be dazzled by the whizzing automobiles and planes and confounded by hospitals, entering a school would give him a sense of familiarity. A building that children in the community go to at set times of the day and on specific days of the week, with classrooms and teachers at the front lecturing students seated in rows and taking notes, would look very much the same as a school 100 years ago.[7]

This, of course, is not entirely true. If Rip van Winkle stepped into an average U.S. elementary school, he would find a richer diversity of children present than there were 100 years ago—not only girls and boys, and white and black children, but also kids from all socioeconomic classes and geographies. Children's lessons would feature more cognitively demanding content on subjects such as reading and mathematics, and the religion-infused values education would largely be missing, with some concepts having been repackaged as character education or social and emotional learning.[8] Instead of managing small classes with more fluid teaching styles, teachers would be instructing a larger number of students, and teaching itself would be more bureaucratic and rationalized.[9]

All the same, the modern teaching and learning model would feel quite familiar to a person from a century ago. The core elements of the "Prussian model," as education scholars call it, have been remarkably stable over time. The rollout of mass schooling has been so closely tied to this model that schools will closely resemble each other no matter where in the world you live. Because of this, some scholars have characterized schools around the world as acting effectively as one "shared global institution."[10] Others point to the role that international institutions, especially those financing educational development in the Global South, have played in disseminating a "common blueprint for schools" over the past five decades.[11] Of course, not all schools follow this common blueprint worldwide, but by and large the schooling experiences of most children share many common characteristics.

In any given country, the average school today shares similar characteristics about where, when, and how children learn. Structurally, children go to school buildings during predetermined times of the day, week, and year, though the total number of hours that children spend in school varies widely by country. In school, children are grouped together by age, and teachers lead these groups through a prescribed curriculum developed by adults with little input from students themselves. Teachers rarely enjoy observation, feedback, or support from their peers. Various subjects are taught in discrete time periods throughout the day, and this structure is seldom altered—in the United States, for example, subject times have remained more or less stable since 1920.[12] Students rely heavily on teacher instruction, with a particular focus on academic subjects, and they work to actively understand and retain the material presented, while frequently being incentivized to do so via examinations administered by their teachers. Recent research observing teaching in U.S. math classrooms demonstrates that many of the teaching techniques, particularly teacher-led instruction, are the same as those described by academics studying teaching in the 1900s.[13] Students progress through school based on their performance within predetermined time periods.

That said, how much of a problem is the persistence of the Prussian model?

## The Twin Problems of Skills Inequality and Skills Uncertainty

Two critical problems are present in the Prussian model's approach to education. First, although mass schooling has spread around the globe in virtually the same form, it reaches and serves some children well and others poorly. Second, the model's rigidities are at risk of holding back students from developing the skills required to succeed in a fast-changing world.

### *Skills Inequality and the 100-Year Gap*

Among and within countries, there are deep inequalities in what schools help children learn, know, and do. Many children may not make it to the schoolhouse door in the first place, and still others are not mastering the foundational skills they need for future work, learning, and life. Children from all socioeconomic backgrounds are affected, but the poorest children carry the heaviest burden. Worse yet, it will take approximately 100 years for those furthest behind to catch up.[14]

**Inequality among and within Countries**   This pressing problem of skills inequality is well documented, most recently by the International Commission on Financing Global Education Opportunity (hereafter, the Education Commission). Through careful analysis of education data globally, the Education Commission has projected that by 2030 more than half the world's 2 billion children will not be on track to achieve basic secondary-level skills, including literacy, numeracy, problem solving, and critical thinking.[15] As figure 1-1 shows, many of the children missing out on a quality education live in high-income countries, where nearly 1 in 3 children will be left behind. But children are especially poorly served in low-income countries, where 9 out of every 10 children are projected to reach adulthood without the skills they need to thrive.[16]

Additionally, most countries, regardless of average education performance or country income level, struggle with deep education inequalities

**FIGURE 1-1**   Projected Learning Outcomes in 2030

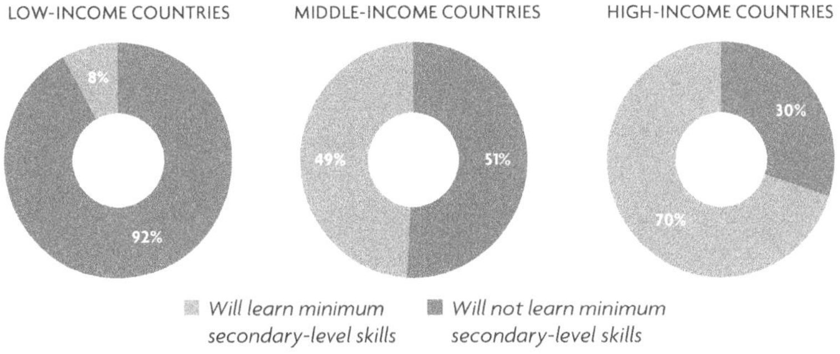

LOW-INCOME COUNTRIES          MIDDLE-INCOME COUNTRIES          HIGH-INCOME COUNTRIES

8%

92%

49%   51%

30%

70%

☐ Will learn minimum          ■ Will not learn minimum
   secondary-level skills          secondary-level skills

*Source:* International Commission on Financing Global Education Opportunity, *The Learning Generation: Investing in Education for a Changing World* (New York: International Commission on Financing Global Education Opportunity, 2016), p. 68.

between their rich and poor students.[17] For example, on the secondary-school mathematics proficiency examination under the Program for International Student Assessment (PISA), the global gap between rich and poor students is 57 percent. The United States is home to the widest gap, of almost 40 percentage points, in students achieving high levels of math proficiency: two-thirds of the richest children reach proficiency levels 3 and 4, compared with only about a quarter of the poorest.[18] This inequality starts early in the child's life. In the United States, scholars have found that "upon entering kindergarten, children from low-income families have weaker academic and attention skills, on average, and a higher probability of demonstrating antisocial behavior than children from higher-income families. None of these gaps shrinks over the course of elementary school."[19] This entrenched disparity is also evident across the developing world. For example, at the primary level in Morocco, only 24 percent of low- and middle-income students meet basic math proficiency benchmarks, yet the richest children achieve these basic levels at nearly double this rate.[20]

Some evidence suggests that this skills gap may be smaller for non-academic skills. A 2012 PISA study on creative problem solving, for example, demonstrated that the socioeconomic status of learners affected their creative problem-solving scores to a lesser extent than it did for math, literacy, or science.[21] Overall, however, the education community does not yet have the tools to take summative and broadly comparable measures of nonacademic skills.[22]

The problem of skills inequality, however, is not simply one of magnitude; it also asymmetrically persists over time. In any developed nation, a century ago the average adult had completed about 4.5 years of schooling and just over a third of youth were in enrolled in secondary school. But these levels of access and attainment are not a relic of the past, as these results are comparable to the educational levels of adults and children in the developing world today.

**The 100-Year Gap**  In *Why Wait 100 Years? Bridging the Gap in Global Education*, we argued that, at the current pace of change, skills inequality will not be redressed anytime soon. In fact, it would take approximately a hundred years for girls and boys in poor countries to catch up to today's education levels in rich countries.[23] This slow pace of change is just as evident between poor and rich communities within countries and regions. For instance, although all of the richest boys in the countries of sub-Saharan Africa are expected to achieve secondary school completion by 2041, the poorest girls will need 70 additional years to reach that milestone.[24] Extensive studies of educational inequality in the United States also highlight the alarming slowness of efforts to close the high- and low-income gap in achievement scores, social and emotional skills, and college completion.[25] At current rates, it will take another 60 to 110 years to close the gaps in the academic and behavioral competencies between high- and low-income children entering kindergarten today.[26]

With our current pace of change, deep inequalities in both access to and the quality of education will be with us for some time to come. The promise of education as the equalizer, helping to compensate for social and economic differences, seems far from many children's reality.

**The Problems of Access and Quality**  This inequality in skills development persists both within and among countries for a number of reasons. Some are related to children's lives outside school, such as their nutritional status, the level of stress or support they experience on a daily basis, their family resources, the educational levels of their parents, and their health and emotional well-being. Other factors include how well school systems themselves adapt to children's needs, such as efforts to accommodate hard-to-reach populations and to consistently deliver a quality teaching and learning experience.

Yet even if schools provide such an open learning environment, many children around the world never even make it to the school door—or, if they do, they stay for only a few years. Today, approximately 263 million youth between ages 6 and 17 are out of school, a number that has remained the same for a decade. Different approaches are needed to reach these "last-mile" children.[27] They face multiple barriers to access, including the intersecting disadvantages of poverty, gender, and location. For the world's poorest families, children who are in school cannot provide either labor or income on the days when the family needs help farming, and girls who are in school cannot provide childcare for their younger siblings.[28] And though most countries have abolished school fees, poor families often face prohibitive indirect costs for materials such as uniforms and books.[29] Displacement, armed conflict, and insecurity can leave children without education for years, even decades; children living in regions affected by humanitarian emergencies account for half the world's out-of-school population.[30]

Even the young people enrolled in and attending school may be learning little while they are there. For a number of countries, the economist Lant Pritchett has documented the flat "learning achievement profile" of students: for every year spent in school, the amount that students have learned in subjects like literacy, numeracy, and science barely increases.[31] These flat or nearly flat learning achievement profiles are tragically widespread. The Education Commission estimates that of all the children who will not be on track to achieve basic learning outcomes in 2030, roughly three-quarters are actually in school—they simply are not learning.[32] (These estimates do not even include broader skills such as flexibility or collaboration, where there are limited reliable cross-national data.) Lack of learning also contributes to higher dropout rates; in Latin America, for instance, an alarming near 50 percent of boys are dropping out of secondary school, in part because the quality of education is so low.[33]

This phenomenon of students' low learning levels has many causes. According to the UNESCO Institute for Statistics, in 2015 the developing world had a deficit of 2.7 million primary school teachers. If this trend were to continue, by 2030 more than 25 million new teachers would need to be recruited just to ensure that every child can attend primary school.[34] In many countries, including some of the poorest, teachers are so over-burdened that they are teaching classes of 60 or more students at a time, with 10 students for every book and children squeezed onto benches.[35] These overcrowded classrooms contain students of widely varying levels, providing a further challenge for teachers. Furthermore, especially in the developing world, teachers are burdened with nonteaching duties including administration and event planning, and so they frequently may not be in the classroom and actually teaching.[36] In many African countries, for example, students receive just under three hours of instruction each day.[37] The language of instruction and pedagogical approaches used in the classroom also limit student learning. All over the world, almost 40 percent of children are not taught in their native language, despite evidence showing that mother-tongue instruction is more effective for learning.[38] In India, differentiated instruction—tailoring lessons to children's different levels of understanding—has been shown to be feasible and effective with the approach of teachers who are "teaching at the right level," but most classrooms are not using this method.[39] Many students also have learning or physical disabilities that are not accommodated, and schools lack accessible materials and teachers trained to teach special needs students.[40]

The problems of limited access to school and poor-quality schooling hit our poorest young people most heavily. We must give serious thought to how education can help support these children, not within the next 100 years but within the next decade.

*Skills Uncertainty: Preparing Children for a Changing World*

The magnitude of this 100-year gap becomes more daunting when you consider that it is between what we consider to be a good or a bad education today, and does not even consider the type of education that children will need for the future. In addition to the limitations of weak schooling systems in effectively reaching and teaching all children essential academic skills, many are wondering if the Prussian model itself is limiting the relevance of a school-based education in a fast-changing world.

**A Fast-Changing World**    Today, people and ideas are flowing across borders at a greater speed than ever before in human history. Technology is becoming omnipresent. The gig economy is on the rise. Even though not every child lives in a community where this is true, the pace of change is so rapid that it soon may be the case. Children who struggle to learn their academic subjects in weak schools, and also children who are effectively mastering the curriculum in strong schools, will need to be well equipped with a wide range of skills—from critically reading texts and collaboratively solving problems to quickly adapting to new forces affecting the economy, society, and the natural environment.

The pace of change in society, from technological innovation to global interconnectedness, stands in stark contrast to the pace of change in school systems. In the past decade, mobile phone service—and with it, access to information—has spread faster across most of Africa than the infrastructure supporting transportation, clean water, and sewerage put together.[41] Advances in artificial intelligence and robotics are happening faster than many scientists have predicted.[42] Social institutions, which take on average 10 to 15 years to adapt, are not keeping up with the rapid pace of innovation. Undoubtedly, societies have always faced changes, but the journalist Thomas Friedman provides a pithy comparison to illustrate the increasing speed of change: 100 years ago, new technologies like airplanes and automobiles took 20 years to significantly change our world, but today's new technologies such as smartphones take approximately 5 to 7 years to transform our daily lives.[43]

**New Skills for New Work**    This rapid social change translates into major shifts in the world of work, not least in the skills demanded by employers. Historically, economists, employers, and policymakers have tended to understand changing skill demands as an issue of educational attainment. As technology evolves, conventional wisdom dictates that employers demand more sophisticated sorts of skills; in response to such demands, employees must seek progressively higher levels of education to amass the skills needed to compete effectively in the labor market. In general, this understanding of educational supply and demand has explained the economic response to technological change over the past decade.[44]

However, given the rapid pace of technological change so far in the

21st century, many researchers have been looking into the factors that underlie education's ability to respond to shifting skill demands.[45] Central to this work is uncovering which specific skills employers demand. In their seminal 2003 work, economists David Autor, Frank Levy, and Richard Murnane of MIT and Harvard analyzed skill demands in terms of tasks performed, mapped in relation to the tasks computers were capable of executing at the time. They evaluated tasks on two dimensions: cognitive versus manual, and routine versus nonroutine.[46] On these dimensions, the researchers found that nonroutine cognitive tasks became increasingly important to employers between 1960 and 1998, just as routine tasks, which can be completed with discrete, programmable rules, declined in importance. In practice, this means that demand for workers who are able to perform nonroutine tasks—those that require flexibility, creativity, and complex communication, among other skills—increased. Accordingly, companies have increasingly turned to education institutions for a supply of employees whose nonroutine cognitive skills complement the routine task performance of modern technology.

Many other studies have built on this original analysis. For example, recent workforce research by such organizations as the McKinsey Global Institute, World Economic Forum, and the Organization for Economic Cooperation and Development (OECD) echo the 2003 findings of Autor, Levy, and Murnane: as machines increasingly are able to perform sophisticated routine tasks, the labor market increasingly demands an expanded suite of skills for nonroutine job functions.[47] Such studies have relied on national and international economic data as well as interviews with leading industry professionals, have explored the cognitive dimension of employability, and have highlighted the high cognitive demand of the modern market.[48]

As the specter of automation looms ever larger, researchers have moved to assess additional skills dimensions involved in the changing world of work. Chief among these are intrapersonal and interpersonal skills, often called "noncognitive" or "soft" skills by employers and academics.[49] Though psychologists and sociologists have long written about the role of intrapersonal and interpersonal skills in employability, it was not until recently that economists began to research how they are linked.[50] In particular, University of Chicago economist James Heckman and his colleagues have shown that noncognitive abilities matter for employability—and, perhaps more important, that these abilities can be developed through targeted policy interventions.[51] Reports on employability often complement their discussion of growing cognitive demands with the observation that noncognitive skills—particularly in interpersonal communication—are becoming more important in the world of work.[52]

In the past several years, multiple studies have examined the discrete skills needed for the future of work. Among these is a new report that points to the growing demand for a range of interpersonal and cognitive skills, including social perceptiveness, systems analysis, originality, and teaching.[53] Exploring the digitalization of the American economy, Mark Muro, Sifan Liu, Jacob Whiton, and Siddaharth Kulkarni of the Metropolitan Policy Program at Brookings highlight a different piece of work readiness: the increasing demand for digital skills, from using word processing software to writing elaborate codes.[54] In some respects, though, it is impossible to forecast the precise skills needed for the future of work, as it is difficult to predict how technology will develop even five years from now—not to mention the 10- and 20-year projections that education systems will need to prepare today's learners. Still, a strong theme emerges from this wealth of skills research: the future of work will require a broad range of competencies and abilities, from cognitive and interpersonal or intrapersonal skills to digital fluency.

In practice, this means that workers will need to coexist with and complement machines that perform routine tasks by leveraging their interpersonal and complex problem-solving competencies.[55] The OECD estimates that even though few jobs are at risk of being completely automated, most workers will see 50 to 70 percent of their tasks lost to automation.[56] Nurse technicians, for example, might be stripped of routine tasks such as taking vital signs; instead, they will be expected to engage with the patient, convey subtleties of the patient's expressions to a physician, and solve problems when machine errors occur.[57]

In a series of reports on skills in the workforce, the World Economic Forum stressed the magnitude of these changing skills demands, noting that "on average, by 2020, more than a third of the desired core skill sets of most occupations will be comprised of skills that are not yet considered crucial to the job today."[58] For example, in South Africa, one report estimates that 39 percent of core job skills across all industries will have completely changed by 2020, placing heavy demand on such skills as flexibility, information and communications technology (ICT) knowledge, and emotional intelligence.[59] In the United States, the fastest-growing jobs over the past 30 years have been those that require high levels of both math and social skills, such as physicians and management analysts.[60]

Over the past decade, leaders around the globe have been vocal in their disappointment with how education systems are preparing youth for this changing world of work. In a recent study, only 53 percent of industry leaders said that they are even reasonably confident in their companies' ability to recruit and train workers who match the diversity of future skills needs.[61] Automation has hollowed out the labor market, leaving many middle-skilled workers out of work or in low-wage jobs, a phenomenon documented in more than 30 countries across the developed and developing worlds.[62] Conversely, employers are struggling to find people with the skills that are uniquely human and complement digital technologies, such as communication, teamwork, critical thinking, and flexibility. A 70-country study by the McKinsey Global Institute estimates that by 2020, approximately 83 million high- and middle-skilled jobs will go unfilled because employers looking to hire in developed and developing countries will not be able to find people with the necessary academic and nonacademic skills.[63]

**Educating Global Citizens**   As shown above, discussion of skills gaps tends to revolve around the demands of one group: employers. Increasingly, however, the demand for an expanded suite of skills is being discussed beyond the boardroom. From media outlets to parent organizations, stakeholders around the world are racing to determine the skills we need to thrive in what some have termed a "post-truth" era.[64] Civic leaders and policymakers regularly argue that we must equip young people with complex cognitive and interpersonal skills like critical literacy not simply because employers demand it, but because such abilities are required for productive citizenship in an increasingly complex, interconnected, and fast-changing world. Leaders recognize that education experiences must prepare them to solve society's problems, which cut across borders and range from climate change and migration to violent extremism.[65]

In *Teaching and Learning for the Twenty-First Century,* Fernando Reimers and Connie Chung of the Harvard Graduate School of Education argue that, despite global ambitions, education systems are not creating sufficient opportunities for youth to learn these skills.[66] Case studies evaluating education planning in six nations reveal that education systems around the globe are unequipped to target 21st-century competencies and prepare children to be constructive global citizens. The academic Yong Zhao argues that for education to truly help students flourish in the modern working world, it should foster their entrepreneurial spirit, from curiosity to creativity to resilience—and yet, he argues, the structure of mass schooling rarely does this. The better countries do on the PISA, Zhao says, the worse they tend to score in entrepreneurial capacity, as measured by the Global Entrepreneurship Monitor's annual global survey on entrepreneurship.[67] Building on Zhao's work, analysts at A. T. Kearney found that top PISA-scoring countries had an average perceived entrepreneurial capability score of 0.06, almost half that of mid- and low-scoring countries on PISA, which had an average score of 0.13.[68]

**Life-Long Learning**   All of these factors and more are coming together to change how our children will live, work, and create.[69] These changes also have deep implications for how we should educate them. Of course, all young people will need to develop a deep mastery of academic skills, from math to science to languages to history. However, such skills are by no means the full range of capabilities that young people must develop to be successful in their adult lives. Children who have access to good schools and can master the basics, as well as children who are not mastering the basics, will need to be prepared to continue to learn, adapt, create, and innovate throughout their lives. Simply put, young people today will need to develop the competencies that allow them to be life-long learners: they must acquire the knowledge and skills needed to effectively manipulate and use their knowledge in ever-changing contexts. Although this set of broad competencies has always been useful for young people, the central challenge for children today lies in navigating uncertainty, complexity, and rapid change. The question for education is whether it can enable our children to meet these challenges.

*Three*

# What Do We Mean by Leapfrogging?

## Three Cheers for the Industrial Era's Model of Schooling

Given the radical changes afoot, does this mean that we should abandon the Prussian model of schooling altogether? Education debates today commonly call for education policy to depart from the industrial model of schooling. This call comes from all corners of the globe, from the United States to Brazil to Nigeria to India. Educators, nonprofit leaders, technologists, investors, academics, and even some policymakers call for "reinventing" and "reimagining" education.[1] The mass schooling model that is so globally pervasive is said to be broken, an artifact of the 19th century that privileged uniformity at scale and is no longer suitable in a fast-changing digital and globalized world.

But what exactly do educators mean when they argue that we need to shed our current schooling model for a new one, and is it a good idea? In fact, many characteristics of today's mass education approach were revolutionary when they were developed and continue to be worthwhile two centuries later. Taking stock of those workable aspects, while also trying to understand and evaluate the possibilities for reinvention, is important to keep from throwing the proverbial baby out with the bathwater—a phenomenon not unknown in education.

At its core, the mass schooling movement is a radical enterprise in social equality. In our effort to reimagine the industrial era's model of schooling, we should not lose the central principle that every child is equally entitled to a quality education. Today, virtually every society has a schooling system where governments and families accept that going to school should be a part of every young person's childhood. As the scholar Marcelo M. Suárez-Orozco puts it, "For the first time in human history, basic education in formal schools has become a normative ideal the world over."[2] Perhaps most important, this commitment to the right to education for all has led to significant social benefits.

This spread of schooling around the globe has had many positive outcomes, not only for the individuals who have been educated but also for societies overall. The world is healthier than it has ever been. Two hundred years ago, people lived to be an average of less than 40 years old. Today, the average person lives to be 71.[3] Education—of girls and women in particular—has played an important role in improving global health. Health researchers have found that, since 1970, "of the 8.2 million more children who survived past age five, increases in women's educational attainment led to 4.2 million of them."[4] Increases in girls' education have also played an important role in combating HIV/AIDS and malaria; because of education's effectiveness alongside medical interventions, it is often referred to as a "social vaccine" for these health epidemics.[5]

The world is also vastly wealthier, and for the first time in human history experts estimate that extreme poverty can be nearly eliminated by 2030. In recent years, the percentage of people in extreme poverty has fallen below 10 percent of the world's population, which is an especially staggering finding given that half the planet's population lived in extreme poverty only a few decades ago.[6] Mass schooling has contributed significantly to this rise in welfare. In the United States, for example, increasing education levels since the 19th century are estimated to account for between one-fifth and one-third of economic growth.[7] Globally, from 1950 to 2010, each additional year of schooling in the population increased economic growth by 5 to 12 percent.[8]

Today's educated populations are also driving the economic models of the future. Crowdsourcing, which taps into the time and talents of the many to accomplish quickly what previously was done slowly by the few, is changing everything from evaluating patents to tracking endangered species to designing T-shirts. Jeff Howe, who coined the term "crowdsourcing," argues that this online phenomenon is possible only because of today's high education levels in many populations and their ability to connect with each other virtually.[9]

The scaling-up of mass education has also affected women's ability to work outside the home. Consider the systems that working parents, and especially mothers, would need to have in place to care for their children if schools did not exist. The childcare provided during the school day, combined with expanded opportunity in the labor market, allowed increasing numbers of women to enter the workforce.[10] As more women left home to seek employment, families became increasingly dependent on schools to care for their children—a self-perpetuating cycle that bolstered demand for and further cemented the place of mass schooling.[11] Indeed, in many countries schooling continues to provide a backbone of childcare that enables parents, especially women, to actively participate in the labor market.

Perhaps one of the most fundamental contributions of mass schooling has been to shift social identities from tribal to national lines. Mass schooling has helped shape citizens' identities through a common curriculum and shared sense of history, a shared language with which to communicate, and a set of values that spreads across groups within a country. The philosopher Benedict Anderson described this phenomenon as developing "imagined communities"—"deep, horizontal comradeship" with others whom an individual may never meet within the national boundaries.[12] Depending on the content, values, and structures of mass schooling, this influence can be either a good or bad thing. Education can reinforce social dynamics that foster civic discourse, inclusion, and diversity—or do just the opposite.[13] However, in many (if by no means all) parts of the world, mass schooling has helped foster more peaceful, democratic, and just societies.[14] If the right to mass education is enjoyed equitably across a population, it has been shown to have a pacifying effect, markedly reducing a country's risk of civil strife and war.[15]

There are many past and present reasons to admire the global project of mass schooling. The question then remains, what precisely is it that educators and innovators are so eager to reinvent?

## Two Pillars for Transforming Education:
## What and How Children Learn

The answer is twofold. First, what children learn in school—the academic skills that are central in most schools around the globe—may be only part of the skills that young people need to thrive in this fast-changing world. Second, how children are learning in school aligns poorly with how they learn best and, crucially, how they develop the full range of skills they will need in the future.

### *What Should Students Learn? The Breadth-of-Skills Movement*

Many educators argue that the best way for schools to prepare young people for future success is to help them develop a broad range of learning, work, and life skills that they can deploy all their lives, regardless of what the future entails.[16] This does not mean jettisoning academic learning, but it does mean using teaching and learning approaches that enable students to deeply delve into subjects while also fostering a range of what some refer to as "21st-century skills." At the core, education systems must move from prioritizing knowledge acquisition to prioritizing both knowledge acquisition and the development of skills needed to use that knowledge effectively in new contexts over time. Frameworks that set out a vision for 21st-century skills often present a balanced vision of a breadth of skills or broad range of skills, including academic subjects, globally relevant topics, intrapersonal skills (which include things like emotional intelligence), and interpersonal skills (which include listening and interacting with others).

For example, in 2008 Australia put forward a new national curriculum to better prepare its students for learning, work, and life. The curriculum sets out seven general capabilities that guide teaching and learning in the schools: literacy, numeracy, ICT capability, critical and creative thinking, personal and social responsibility, ethical understanding, and intercultural understanding. These general capabilities may not reflect all the distinct subjects taught in the classroom, but they guide the teaching and learning process inside schools in the hope that students will become "confident and creative individuals" and "active and informed citizens."[17] Today, hundreds of frameworks—developed by academics, practitioners, policymakers, and businesses—articulate different conceptualizations of how young people can cultivate this broad range of needed work, learning, and life skills.[18]

The Center for Universal Education (CUE) at Brookings refers to this approach as the *breadth-of-skills movement*. Esther Care and Kate Anderson have described the concept as follows: "Skills are enablers— they provide us with the means to access a multiplicity of mental and physical activities. These skills rely not only on cognition, but also on the interdependencies of cognitive, social, and emotional characteristics. Shifts in skills, away from the narrow focus on literacy and numeracy and toward breadth of skills, are needed to navigate our changing societies and for individuals to function as responsible citizens."[19] The recognition of the importance of the breadth of skills as an educational goal is long-standing and has become widespread. Twenty years ago, for example, the former president of the European Commission, Jacques Delors, chaired UNESCO's International Commission on Education for the Twenty-First Century. The commission's seminal report, often referred to as the Delors Report, argued that education systems must focus on preparing students for life-long learning. To do this, the report stated, young people need not only to learn to know—the focus of most education systems worldwide— but also to learn to do, to live together, and to be.[20]

Academia has long supported this vision of broad skills that includes but builds upon the traditional academic subjects taught in schools. For example, in his 2009 book *Five Minds for the Future*, educational researcher Howard Gardner argued that young people will need five minds—or sets of competencies—"to thrive in the world during the eras to come."[21] The five minds are (1) the disciplined mind, which is able to fully master at least one particular scholarly discipline, craft, or profession; (2) the synthe-sizing mind, which is able to put disparate pieces of information together in a way that makes sense; (3) the creating mind, which develops fresh ways of thinking about things and unexpected answers; (4) the respectful mind, which seeks to understand and work effectively with others; and (5) the ethical mind, which questions the givens in society and considers how citizens can best improve society.[22]

In the words of one innovator, Shankar Maruwada of India's EkStep, this breadth-of-skills movement ultimately seeks "to educate children not for what is needed today but for where the ball will be in the future."[23] It naturally has led more and more people in society to ask if schools are up to this task, echoing a long-standing topic of debate in education circles about how children learn best.

### *How Should Students Learn? The Importance of Student-Centered Approaches*

Long-standing educational traditions have thought deeply about how to align teaching with how children learn best. For example, in Western education, the philosopher Jean-Jacques Rousseau firmly articulated a vision of student-centered pedagogy in the mid-1700s with the publication of *Émile*, his work on the individual's relationship to society and the role of education in children's growth and development. A century later, John Dewey and other education innovators were developing new theories of teaching, reimagining education and starting the progressive education movement. Perhaps one of the most well-known approaches within this movement is the Montessori educational approach developed by Maria Montessori. Larry Page and Sergey Brin, the cofounders of Google, both attended Montessori schools as children and frequently credit this formative education as contributing to their ability to develop their company. The progressive education movement has many different approaches, but what binds them together is that they use different, more student-centered pedagogical approaches than most traditional schools have, and in many ways still do.

Unfortunately, these approaches remain the exception, not the rule. Indeed, evidence shows that today, most students in most countries are in schools that have only a limited use of student-centered learning approaches.

Classroom observations in the developing world point to the pervasive use of teacher-centered pedagogies.[24] In Ethiopia, for example, one study found that student-centered activities account for only 11 percent of class time.[25] A similar study in Cambodia found that 61 percent of class time is devoted to direct student instruction and only 15 percent is used for student-led work.[26] A 2011 report by the UNESCO International Institute for Capacity Building in Africa echoes these findings when looking at how well teachers receive support in the use of student-centered strategies. The institute's meta-analysis of teacher training research concluded that African "teacher preparation programs have generally not adequately integrated [student-centered pedagogy] into the curriculum."[27]

Even in the developed world, teachers rely heavily on teacher-led instruction. In all education systems across the OECD countries, for example, students report using memorization more frequently than learning strategies that involve making connections and finding new ways to solve a problem. Additionally, fewer than 30 percent of students reported experiencing even the most commonly used student-centered teaching strategies: differentiated instruction, in which teachers provide different learning paths for their different students.[28]

A number of studies, including recent work from the OECD and the *Cambridge Handbook of the Learning Sciences*, emphasize that education and teaching broadly are not incorporating recent findings from neuroscience and the learning sciences on how children best learn academic content, as well as cognitive and interpersonal and intrapersonal skills.[29] In the words of one expert, "perhaps the most solid finding to emerge from the learning sciences is that significant change can't be done by fiddling around at the edges of a system that remains instructionist at the core."[30] Recent learning sciences research frequently states that the common practice of teacher-led instruction runs counter to how children naturally learn best.[31]

This body of research provides additional weight and insight to many of the theories of teaching and learning put forth by leading progressive educators, such as John Dewey's work in the United States in the early 1900s and Paulo Friere's work in Brazil in the second half of the century. Supporting student inquiry, grounding learning in the experiences of everyday life, and fostering experimentation are hallmarks of progressive education approaches.[32] These approaches share a commitment to putting the learner at the center of the teaching process, and many also focus on educational experiences that focus not merely on what learners know but what they can do with what they know.[33]

## Defining Leapfrogging in Education

Educational progress around the world has tended to focus sequentially on access, quality, and relevance—in that order. Education systems first aim to get all learners into the classroom before considering whether they are actually learning anything at their desks. It is not until much later— indeed, until quite recently—that policymakers may question the relevance of that learning to students' lives. In the United States, for example, universal access began with the progressive education movement at the turn of the 20th century, which slowly pushed compulsory education laws through statehouses across the nation. It was not until nearly 50 years later that national attention turned to the topic of learning quality, as evidenced by the passage of the 1965 Elementary and Secondary Education Act—a piece of legislation in President Lyndon B. Johnson's War on Poverty, intended to close the income-based skills gap.

A similar phenomenon occurred in the developing world, where the inclusion of education in the 1948 Universal Declaration of Human Rights spurred global leaders to prioritize universal school enrollment. The 2000 United Nations Millennium Development Goals sharpened this focus by aiming to enroll every girl and boy in primary school. In the past decade, as the global community increasingly gained comparable data on student proficiency, policy leaders finally began to focus seriously on how much—or, in many cases, how little—children learn while in school. It was not until the ratification of the 2015 Sustainable Development Goals, which explicitly articulated the need for learners to develop diverse skills and knowledge in pursuit of sustainable development, that the global community finally set out to provide learners with an education relevant to their lives and livelihoods. To achieve the sort of learning that students across the world both need and deserve, we must jettison this stepwise model of educational progress and make room for an entirely new mental model: leapfrogging.

What, therefore, do we mean by leapfrogging in education? Leapfrogging, often described as the ability to jump ahead or make rapid and non-linear progress, is not well defined in the education literature. Sometimes, in the business literature, it is associated with innovation that disrupts existing paradigms rather than sustains them in a different form.[34] More frequently, leapfrogging is used colloquially to describe examples of rapid change. For example, the term "leapfrogging" often appears in relation to telecommunications or banking sectors in the developing world, where certain nations have been able to bypass whole phases of infrastructure and institution building that other countries had to experience. Many African countries, for example, never systematically invested in laying telephone lines, yet today access to mobile phone service on the continent has grown so rapidly that in many cases communities are more likely to be connected to the outside world via mobile phone service than to have access to electricity or running water.[35] The situation is the same for banking: instead of focusing on expanding physical branches to reach the many communities and families who lack access, people across the developing world are relying on mobile money—transfers and payments via text message—which grew out of innovations in Kenya.[36]

In one of the few previous explorations of leapfrogging in education, John Moravec and Arthur Hawkins argue that a true leap is not merely adding new skills to an existing system but rethinking education systems altogether.[37] As a futurist, John Moravec draws on Peter Drucker's work on the rise of the knowledge worker and argues that we are moving into a new economic model that will privilege "nomadic knowledge workers," whom he defines as people who are "creative, imaginative, innovative," and "can work with almost anybody, anytime, anywhere."[38] Although Moravec recognizes that this is not the current context everywhere, he argues that education should leapfrog to a new approach that prepares young people for what he sees as this eventual condition, and he spells out steps to do this along a continuum of education transformation.[39]

This study took inspiration from the overarching idea that rapid and nonlinear progress can be made without following the usual path. Leapfrogging often connotes ideas of skipping over steps to advance along a particular path, but we do not stick narrowly to this idea. Rather, for us leapfrogging is any approach that can rapidly accelerate educational progress, perhaps skipping steps but certainly ending up in a new place altogether. Perhaps the most important part of defining leapfrogging here is identifying our desired end goal. Therefore, we argue that leapfrogging means any practices, whether new or old, that can address skills inequality much more quickly than the current 100-year gap predicts, and any practices that enable us to meet the challenge of skills uncertainty in a rapidly changing world. Ultimately, leapfrogging should set its sights on helping all children develop breadth of skills, no matter if they are currently in or out of school or living in poor or rich communities.

*Four*

# Can We Leapfrog?

## The Education Paradox of Our Time

Having defined leapfrogging, we now face several questions. Is it possible to address both skills inequality and skills uncertainty at the same time? Does focusing attention on one necessarily distract from the other?

This is the educational paradox for our time. As education systems around the world need to be strengthened to deliver their core services, they also simultaneously need to transform what and how children learn. The problem is that the current ways of helping schools better reach and teach the most marginalized often reinforce the education structures that hold students back from developing the breadth of skills they need for 21st-century life. Throughout human history, social institutions responsible for educating young people have always adapted to new eras, but never before on this scale or in so short a time. A central question for us all is how we can change schooling without losing the commitment to the principles of mass education.

Some argue that skills inequality and skills uncertainty cannot be addressed simultaneously.[1] Education systems need to walk before they can run, the argument goes, and thus they should tackle the problems of access, quality, and relevance in that order. Schooling that now leaves large numbers of children outside their doors or that keeps children in school year after year with little progress in developing central reading and math skills instead needs to focus on getting the basics right. Whether in poor countries or poor communities, educators who advocate this strategy claim that there is a real danger in shifting the goal from access and quality to relevance. They worry that a focus on transforming the teaching and learning experience to help students develop a broader range of skills will, however unintentionally, privilege those who are better served today by schools. As a result, the most marginalized will be forgotten, and thus will be less able to master life-changing academic skills such as reading or math. There is a clear rationale to this argument, and those who make it are often deeply committed to helping marginalized children.

The problem with this approach is that there is a high degree of risk that it will maintain a different kind of inequality in the long term. At its core, this argument means that the Prussian model of schooling should be strengthened in areas where it is weak—in poor countries and poor communities—and should be questioned only in areas where it is strong—in rich countries and rich communities. As poor children gain access to schooling that helps them master basic skills, wealthy children will be participating in learning experiences that help them develop the breadth of skills they need.

This is not mere hypothetical conjecture; it is playing out in education policy around the globe. For example, in Madagascar, the government recently developed an education sector plan to address the 30 percent of children who do not finish primary school and the high numbers of children who are not mastering basic literacy and numeracy. As only 15 percent of teachers in the country have received professional training, significant government effort will be needed to train teachers and place them in rural and hard-to-reach communities.[2] Meanwhile, in Finland, educators are taking seriously the prospects of educating children for a changing world. They are not content to rest on their laurels as one of the consistently top-scoring education systems in international measures such as PISA; instead, the government is ushering in reforms that require schools to increase the use of multidisciplinary themes in teaching and thereby move away from traditional subjects as the organizing principle of learning. The Finnish educator Pasi Sahlberg notes that schools have some flexibility in how to integrate this phenomenon-based teaching approach, and thus will be able to draw on all the traditional school subjects to explore a topic such as the European Union or climate change. He also notes that what is potentially more forward-thinking is the requirement that students have a voice in designing the topic and in how their learning is assessed. Set subjects and control by teachers are making way for themes and opportunities for students to use their voices. The reform, Sahlberg argues, is motivated by the recognition "that schools should teach what young people need in their lives."[3]

What will happen to the students entering school in Madagascar 20 years from now? Will they stand any hope of developing the broad range of skills that Finnish students will likely have by then? Or, despite improved access and quality learning, will they again be woefully left behind, missing crucial skills they need to thrive? Most governments aspire to help young people develop the capabilities they will need to flourish regardless of their starting point. In the words of one former African minister of education, Dzingai Mutumbuka of Zimbabwe, "I wanted the children in my country to develop the skills that will make them globally competitive; they are just as capable as children in other parts of the world."[4]

It would be foolish to argue that Madagascar can become like Finland in a decade, not least because of the massive differences in their economies and available financial resources. But Madagascar could equally chart its own course toward helping children get the full range of skills they need. After all, children are natural-born learners—curious, creative, social, and persistent—and this is no less true in Madagascar than it is in Finland. Technology is advancing so quickly that expensive computer laboratories are being replaced by mobile phones, online and offline tablets, and lightweight solar-powered projectors. If Indonesia can be one of the world leaders in startups, and India can do the same in biometric identification, why cannot Madagascar tackle skills inequality and skills uncertainty without following the same steps as Finland? The long, hard work of reforming education governance and resourcing would be important for this journey, but it is by no means enough. An essential part of the process would have to be identifying new ways of educating children—that is, strategies to engage young people in learning opportunities that will help them master academics at the same time as they build their skills for the 21st century. Luckily, these types of approaches are being tried out in both the poorest and wealthiest parts of the world. Being open to taking a different path is perhaps the first step toward leapfrogging. After all, breaking free from dominant logic—entrenched patterns of thought and action—and the resulting tendency to act in accord with past decisions, also known as path dependence, can be one of the biggest barriers to innovation.[5]

## Can Innovation Help Education Leapfrog?

Many countries—rich and poor alike—aspire to help their young people develop a broad range of skills. In a survey of more than 100 countries, CUE found that three-quarters have expressed such desires in their education policies.[6] However, most are long on aspiration and short on planning; only 13 percent appear to have a concrete plan for how to achieve this vision.[7] They are struggling with the paradox of tackling skills inequality while addressing skills uncertainty, a complex task. Indeed, many countries are considering what steps they should take to help their young people develop the full range of academic, interpersonal, and intrapersonal skills they need.[8]

This paradox is the central motivation of this report. Can we address skills inequality and skills uncertainty at the same time? What new ideas and approaches would enable us to do that? What would a pathway for harnessing innovation for leapfrogging look like? Innovative practices are only one potential source of progress; improved delivery of existing education models will make an important contribution. However, this book focuses solely on the universe of education innovation as a key part of the solution.

We first started exploring these questions through our Skills for a Changing World project and then accelerated our work through a research partnership with the International Commission on Financing Education Opportunity (Education Commission). The Education Commission—chaired by the United Nations (UN) secretary-general's special envoy for global education, former British prime minister Gordon Brown—was convened by several heads of state and launched in Oslo in 2015 with Norwegian prime minister Erna Solberg and UN secretary-general Ban Ki-moon. A group of global leaders worked together for a year before putting forward an ambitious blueprint for accelerating global education progress, particularly in the developing world. The report calls for a major scaling-up of global investment to create a "learning generation" whereby all young people will have access to a quality education.[9]

The Education Commission argues that, to accomplish this goal, education systems must both be strengthened and be better at capitalizing on innovative approaches. Its report recommends improving access and quality by pursuing a series of "transformations," including making weak education systems stronger by following the effective policies of the top quarter of the fastest-improving countries as measured by learning outcomes on literacy as well as prioritizing inclusion and scaling up financing. The commission also calls for a transformation in the use of innovative approaches to where, how, and to whom education is delivered. Innovation, the commission argues, is essential to any acceleration of progress: "Education systems must innovate and change rather than just replicate past success," especially because of the evolving nature of skills that young people need and because many countries are "hitting the limits" of what their education systems can achieve.[10]

In the report prepared for the Education Commission with colleagues Timothy Williams and Priya Shankar, we defined innovation as an idea or technology that is a break from previous practice, often new in a particular context even if not new to the world.[11] This continues to be how we conceive of innovations in education, although we have broadened the definition when scanning the landscape of education innovations to capture existing efforts in innovative education practices.

*Five*

# How to Leapfrog

## Overview of the Leapfrog Pathway and the Global Catalog of Education Innovations

If the ultimate goal of leapfrogging as we define it is to transform what and how children learn so that all young people can develop the broad set of skills they need to thrive, then how can innovations help education do this? We answer this question in two ways: by developing a leapfrog pathway based on existing evidence about how to transform what and how children learn, and by scanning the landscape of education innovations to see how they measure up against our leapfrog pathway. We have compiled thousands of innovations in an effort to better understand their collective potential to help leapfrog education. In doing so, we attempt to provide insights to action-oriented governments, civil society organizations, educators, philanthropic investors, and members of the business community who care about helping young people develop the breadth of skills they need to thrive. We hope that the leapfrog pathway and its corresponding catalog of innovations can illuminate the horizon, showing not only what educational transformation may look like in the future but also what practical action for advancing leapfrogging could look like today. To do so, we first describe how we developed both the leapfrog pathway and the innovations catalog. Second, we give a detailed description of the leapfrog pathway itself, which relies on examples from the catalog to illustrate its different elements.

This exploratory study focuses specifically on the role of innovations in helping education leapfrog. In particular, we have focused on learning about what we are calling the "education innovation community," namely, the many actors who are engaged in supporting innovative education practices worldwide. The leapfrog pathway itself is based on existing evidence around how to transform what and how children learn. Although we developed the leapfrog pathway before finalizing the catalog, both endeavors influenced each other, and many research activities such as literature reviews, interviews, and consultations informed both efforts.

## *The Leapfrog Pathway*

We developed the leapfrog pathway to help identify how education could meet the vision of leapfrogging—accelerating progress to address both skills inequality and skills uncertainty. We based the elements of the pathway on existing evidence about how to transform both what and how children learn, informed by a number of sources—the existing literature on learning and education, as well as innovation and leapfrogging; more than 100 interviews with thought leaders, innovators, and practitioners; and a series of consultations, including with decisionmakers across all levels of education, from ministers of education to teachers.[1]

Although many possible elements could have been included in the pathway—indeed, our initial draft had more than 12—we chose to prioritize the ones most essential to addressing skills inequality and skills uncertainty, and thus to achieving our leapfrogging goal. The pathway has two main parts. First, it identifies strategies to improve the two core elements for leapfrogging: teaching and learning, and the recognition of learning. This means that education cannot leapfrog without attending to these essential elements; it also means that the elements are closely aligned. The pathway's second part identifies support elements, namely including more diverse people and places, and leveraging technology and data. These elements are not necessary for core element transformations, but they are useful tools to consider given the scope and scale of the education challenges we face. The core and support elements focus exclusively on transformations in supplying education, meaning what changes actors delivering education services can make. They do not examine the demand-side forces for leapfrogging education, namely the interest and willingness of actors consuming education services, from students to their parents, to participate in services that use leapfrog approaches. We excluded demand-side factors for leapfrogging simply because of the time constraints of our study, not because we did not consider them important aspects of leapfrogging.

For those considering leapfrogging, the optimal approach will depend heavily on the starting context. Though all nations should aspire to tackle both skills inequality and uncertainty, it will be a meaningful leap to close the current 100-year gap faster than predicted. For out-of-school children in South Sudan, for example, the Can't Wait to Learn program is a major advancement. This intervention, which provides literacy and numeracy training through games and exercises via offline tablets and a community facilitator, helps to address South Sudanese skills inequality. However, it would be unlikely to drastically accelerate progress for children in Argentina, most of whom are already in primary school and mastering basic literacy and numeracy. The Can't Wait to Learn program itself, for that matter, has not been designed to help learners develop the full breadth of skills.

Although an innovation like the Can't Wait to Learn program does not tackle skills inequality and skills uncertainty at the same time, it still significantly accelerates progress in closing the 100-year gap in South Sudan: a hop, one might say, on the way to leapfrogging. An intervention like Can't Wait to Learn could be combined with other efforts that address skills uncertainty in ways that truly will allow learners to leapfrog to a full breadth of skills. To account for programs like Can't Wait to Learn, we designed the leapfrog pathway with a range of destinations. Innovations can help education hop, skip, or—if they address both skills inequality and skills uncertainty—leap forward. Across the core and support elements of the pathway, strategies build on each other rather than replace what has come before. The additive nature of the pathway is important, as leapfrogging will require a wide mix of approaches and strategies to address skills inequality and skills uncertainty.

## *The Global Catalog of Education Innovations*

If the leapfrog pathway has a vision for nonlinear progress, how do current education innovations stack up? What is the ultimate goal to which most innovations aspire—do they aim to advance education by hopping, skipping, or leaping forward? How are they going about reaching these goals? As described above, we were interested in grounding the theory about leapfrogging in existing practice that demonstrates what is possible in the here and now.

From the outset, we were aware that multiple organizations are already scanning the landscape of education innovations. These range from Ashoka, which seeks out social innovators and schools that develop young people's skills for social entrepreneurship; to OECD, which looks for government-based innovative practices; to HundrED, which seeks scalable innovations, particularly from teachers and school leaders; to the Results for Development (R4D) Center for Education Innovations, which examines programs in low- and middle-income countries; to the Inter-American Development Bank's Graduate XXI, which seeks out innovations in Latin America; to EdSurge, a U.S.-based education technology product index. We call these organizations, and the nine others we have identified, the "Education Innovation Spotters"—those that are looking at innovative programs, schools, policies, approaches, and tools; collecting information about them; highlighting them; and sometimes funding or supporting them. Because there was no existing catalog that combined the insights of these different organizations in one place, we decided to create our own.

Our method for studying the landscape of education innovation—the education innovation community—was to compile the lists of these Education Innovation Spotters into a catalog and analyze them in relation to our leapfrog pathway. We had to relax our own definition of innovation and be open to the different definitions used by the Innovation Spotters. In the end, we cataloged all practices that the Innovation Spotters had deemed innovative, deferring to their definitions and criteria. This ranged from thorough and specific classifications of innovation, such as those used by the OECD, to more fluid definitions by those who sought to cast a wide net, like the R4D Center for Education Innovations and HundrED's 100 Finland list. The catalog has almost 3,000 innovations spread across developed and developing countries and includes nonprofit programs, government initiatives, and private sector interventions; individual schools and school chains; and specific products and tools. Most focus on K–12 schooling, although youth workforce development and early childhood also are included. The innovations included nascent innovations that have just begun but have no data on their effectiveness, as well as longer-serving innovations that have external evaluations of effectiveness and evidence of the ability to scale up. We searched for Innovation Spotters working in different languages, including Spanish, Portuguese, and Mandarin. However, we primarily worked in English, as this was the language that most of the Innovation Spotters used. As this was an exploratory study, we sought to capture diverse perspectives and so included diverse lists, some of which focus on technology, others on breadth of skills, and others on specific target populations.

Although this global catalog gives good insights into what the education innovation community is doing, it is by no means comprehensive. Other Innovation Spotters are working in languages outside the scope of our study. Perhaps more significantly, the spotters have undoubtedly overlooked some innovation examples, and so our catalog is only as comprehensive as this combined effort.

### *Hop, Skip, Leap: A Leapfrog Pathway for Education*

We now turn to the leapfrog pathway itself (figure 5-1). After presenting the full pathway, we discuss each of the core and support elements, illustrating features of innovations that could support a hop, skip, or leap with examples of innovations from the catalog (boxes 5-1 and 5-2).

## Core Elements: Increasingly Student-Centered and Individualized

On first glance, it is a scene more befitting a high-tech corporate headquarters than a public school in urban Brazil. In a cavernous room, firetruck-red concrete flooring throws white cubic stools and curving desks into sharp relief. Flatscreen televisions, fixed on rainbow-painted walls lined

**BOX 5-1   Four Things to Know**
**About the Leapfrog Pathway**

1. *Elements*

   The pathway includes two core elements—teaching and learning, and recognition of learning—and two support elements—people and places, and technology and data. The core elements are essential for transforming what and how children learn. In contrast, the support elements are important (but not essential) tools for supporting the core elements. Each element presents an expanding menu of actions building on and adding to the practices that have come before it.

2. *Evidence*

   The pathway has been developed based in large part on existing evidence on ways to transform what and how children learn.

3. *Context*

   Leapfrogging can take many forms depending on the context. In what we call a hop, for example, innovations could support new ways for out-of-school children to master core academic content, thereby more rapidly addressing skills inequality than the current pace of change predicts. A leap, however, is one that addresses skills inequality and skills uncertainty at the same time. We describe three anchor points in the leapfrog pathway—hop, skip, leap—to illustrate but not prescribe the range of possible destinations.

4. *Purpose*

   The pathway was developed not to evaluate individual innovations but rather to help understand the collective efforts of the education innovation community. For example, two separate innovations might not be able to help leapfrog education, but they could do so when working alongside each other.

**BOX 5-2  Five Things to Know about the Global
Catalog of Education Innovations**

1.  *Who, what, where*

    The nearly 3,000 innovations in the catalog come from developed and developing countries and include nonprofit, government, and private sector programs; individual schools and school chains; and specific products and tools. Most focus on K–12 schooling, but some include youth workforce development or early childhood programming.

2.  *Source of data*

    In cataloging and analyzing each innovation in relation to our leapfrog pathway, we relied on publicly available information. Consequently, our information is only as current or complete as the provider's website or external information sources allow.

3.  *Innovation Spotters*

    To compllile our catalog, we used data from 16 organizations. These groups, which we call Innovation Spotters, maintain lists of education innovations from around the world—166 countries in total. Together, these innovations provide insight into what we are calling the education innovation community: the constellation of actors around the globe who are supporting innovative education practices.

4.  *Defining innovation*

    In developing the catalog, we relied entirely on the definitions of innovation that the 16 Innovation Spotters used to develop their lists. The catalog features diverse innovations, from promising to proven and from small to large scale.

5.  *A snapshot of the universe*

    The catalog provides a diverse, useful picture of the education innovation community. But it is a partial one, and by no means represents the universe of education innovations.

FIGURE 5-1  The Leapfrog Pathway for Education

# CORE ELEMENTS

### Teaching and Learning: Increasingly Student-centered

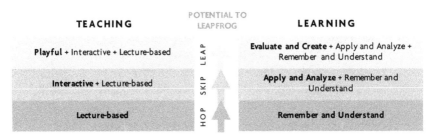

### Recognition of Learning: Increasingly Individualized

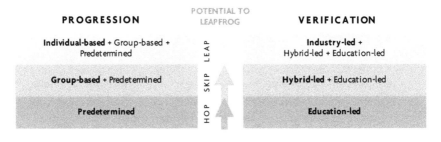

---

# SUPPORT ELEMENTS

### People and Places: Increasingly Diverse

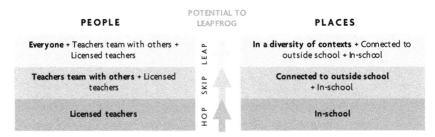

### Technology and Data: Increasingly Results Oriented

| TECHNOLOGY | POTENTIAL TO LEAPFROG | DATA |
|---|---|---|
| **Modification and redefinition** + Augmentation + Substitution | LEAP | **Data for transforming learning experiences** + Data for program improvement + Data for compliance |
| **Augmentation** + Substitution | SKIP | **Data for program improvement** + Data for compliance |
| **Substitution** | HOP | **Data for compliance** |

with corrugated iron, display looping montages of video game footage. Behind two-story glass walls are rows of whiteboards adorned with schematics detailing the construction of towering robots and high-speed jets. And huddled around the computers that fill the rooms, groups of polo-clad teenagers laugh and smile as they tap out the digital codes that will one day become the next great app.

But this is not just any school. At the Núcleo Avançado em Educação (Advanced Education Center; NAVE), secondary-age students learn to create and innovate for work in a digital world. In partnership with Oi Futuro, the social responsibility arm of the Brazilian telecom giant Oi, the state governments of Rio de Janeiro and Pernambuco dreamed up a new model of technical education—one that unites academically rigorous secondary programming with vocational coursework related to the digital economy. Over three years, students in these free, state-run high schools develop expertise in one of three specializations: digital game design, multimedia design, or digital scriptwriting.

Applied, project-based work is the name of the game at NAVE. Lessons regularly require students to deploy their digital literacy, creativity, and entrepreneurship alongside academic learning, as teachers task students with designing and publishing applications, games, and other digital products for public consumption. In math class, for example, ninth-grader Ana assumes the role of a digital scriptwriter, leading her team to create an app-based game for learning geometry.

"Japanese architecture is filled with squares and triangles," she says, sketching polygons in her notebook. "What if players had to fight in a sort of geometry dojo?" Her teammates nod enthusiastically as she speaks. João, the multimedia designer, immediately switches on his laptop and begins sketching a box-shaped ninja. Meanwhile, Enzo, the game designer, shows Ana the various code sequences that they might use to populate a digital dojo with random shapes. At the end-of-unit game festival, she presents the game to her parents: a geometric reasoning puzzle where players, taking the role of a box-shaped ninja, must outrun triangular samurais and collect the geometric pieces that form the key to the dojo's exit. Months later, their game, KAM, would be featured at the Tenth Annual Brazilian Symposium of Games and Digital Entertainment.

Despite its firm grounding in the digital age, however, NAVE does not eschew analog learning. Down the hall, in an interdisciplinary workshop, teams of learners lounge on bright red beanbags as they play student-created board games on topics ranging from chemistry to civics. In one corner, a group of young boys take turns building life-saving medicinal compounds out of chemistry playing cards. In another, students take the role of various historical figures and must reach consensus on a particular political debate in order to advance on the board. Teachers circulate through the room, pushing students to articulate what they learned and connecting game discussions back to classroom topics.

NAVE highlights what it takes to prepare youth for work in the digital age. Students must be challenged to apply their digital literacy skills, and core academic learning must be brought to life as a tool for meaningful creation. This, of course, requires playful learning. NAVE shows that playful learning can produce incredible results, even on academic metrics of student success: the two NAVE technical and vocational high schools in Rio de Janeiro and Pernambuco scored first among all public schools in their respective states on the national secondary leaving exam.[2]

Central to addressing skills inequality and skills uncertainty is transforming what and how children learn. The NAVE schools in Brazil are one example of how to transform teaching and learning. Nevertheless, this cannot be done without focusing on how students' learning is recognized both within schools and outside them. These core elements of the leapfrog pathway are closely related, and leaping forward in one element often means a similar shift in another element. We examine both in turn.

### *Teaching and Learning: Increasingly Student-Centered*

How students learn and how teachers teach are at the core of an education system's ability to develop student skills. Studies across the world have demonstrated repeatedly that changes in teaching practice improve student learning more than any other school-based interventions. In the developing world, studies have shown that the most effective educational programming is focused on promoting evidence-based pedagogies.[3] In the developed world, John Hattie combined over 1,200 meta-analyses and found that, compared with other interventions, changes in teaching and learning most positively influenced student achievement.[4] Additionally, the International Initiative for Impact Evaluation's review of educational programming identified structured pedagogy, which integrates evidence-based instructional approaches, as having the largest and most consistent impact on learning outcomes.[5]

Teaching and learning experiences that lead with students' interests and needs are more effective and enable a greater range of skill development.[6] Underpinning this finding from the learning sciences is the idea that how teachers teach ultimately helps shape what skills students are able to develop. Although some important 21st-century skills, such as digital literacy, can be taught through teacher-directed instruction, many others cannot. To hone their ability to solve problems collaboratively, for example, children need teaching and learning experiences that give them space to lead, experiment, fail, and try again. Supporting teachers' capacity to guide children's learning is an important part of transforming the teaching and learning process (figure 5-2).

Leapfrogging in education requires being open to new ways of teaching and learning that may seem different from those found in the average classroom. Teaching and learning experiences that put students at the center, fostering their natural inquisitiveness and exposing them to important topics that will shape their lives, are important for transforming education. In the words of John Dewey: "If we teach students the same way as yesterday, we rob them of tomorrow."[7]

**Teaching**   Effective teaching puts student inquiry at the center and actively engages students in "doing things and thinking about the things they are doing."[8] This overarching principle is the driving force behind a collection of diverse pedagogical approaches. These teaching strategies frequently recognize that children are natural-born learners, often citing the important role that active student inquiry has in developing skills and capacities. Some pedagogical approaches entail harnessing children's innate ability to play as a way of helpings students "actively [engage] in meaningful discovery" and allowing them the freedom to experiment and explore problems.[9] Others focus on connecting classroom learning to students' everyday lives, including pedagogies in which learners participate in real-life activities, such as internships and community projects, and learn

**FIGURE 5-2** Teaching and Learning: Increasingly Student-Centered

| TEACHING | POTENTIAL TO LEAPFROG | LEARNING |

### TEACHING

Lecture-based +
Interactive +

**PLAYFUL:**
Learning is driven by students' inquiry and needs, meaningfully connected to their lives, and fosters experimentation and social interaction. Teachers often act as facilitators and guides.

Lecture-based +

**INTERACTIVE:**
Teacher is in charge, and sometimes engages students in discussion, activities, or group-based work.

**LECTURE-BASED:**
Teacher is in charge; students passively receive information.

### POTENTIAL TO LEAPFROG

LEAP

SKIP

HOP

### LEARNING

Remember and understand +
Apply and understand +

**EVALUATE AND CREATE:**
Students evaluate, design, and create original work, and question and criticize existing work.

Remember and understand +

**APPLY AND ANALYZE:**
Students apply information in new situations and draw connections among ideas.

**REMEMBER AND UNDERSTAND:**
Students recall facts and basic concepts and explain ideas or concepts.

through reflecting on those experiences.[10] Educators use various terms to describe these approaches—including active learning, experiential learning, and problem-based learning—and each emphasizes a slightly different piece of the teaching and learning process. One term used to describe these pedagogical approaches is "playful learning," because recent definitions have attempted to draw together different elements and bodies of evidence around student-centered learning. For example, in one recent definition, playful learning is described as learning experiences that allow for active student engagement, experimentation and iteration, social interaction, curiosity and joy, and meaningful connection to student experience.[11] The term is also a useful reminder that children are born learning, which they do through playing with people and things almost from the moment they are born. Of course, at any given moment, students may not experience all of these characteristics as they work through tough problems or master challenging skills, and educators have an important role to play in fostering this type of learning experience. Pedagogical practices that foster playful learning range from project-based learning—where children work on an extended project through which they not only master academic skills but also develop intrapersonal and interpersonal skills—to more personal learning experiences where students set their own goals and their learning journey is facilitated through interactions with teachers and peers.

Playful learning goes a step beyond simply making learning interactive, which might focus solely on involving students in activities without requiring conscious engagement or reflection or without allowing room for experimentation and iteration. Additionally, these types of pedagogies regularly tap into student curiosity and interest to drive learning, giving students increased agency over what and how they learn and structuring curricula so that they can discover and produce knowledge for themselves.[12] Learning skills through subjects, as previously mentioned, is another classroom practice that can advance student-led inquiry. Take, for instance, the concrete example of a biology class that allows learners to explore diabetes in their communities. Here, students might develop their analytical writing abilities by drafting a policy brief, practice scientific thinking by designing an experiment, learn communication skills through interacting with community members, and practice taking another person's perspective when talking with patients—all the while gaining expertise on the function of human kidneys.[13]

Pedagogical approaches that characterize playful learning enjoy wide empirical support, with studies consistently demonstrating that they result in better student outcomes than do traditional pedagogies.[14] Research has shown, too, that these types of pedagogical approaches can effectively foster important noncognitive skills. In an extensive review of evidence on learning, Hilton and Pellegrino's 2012 report to the National Research Council finds that practices similar to those detailed above support both content knowledge acquisition and the development of interpersonal and intrapersonal skills.[15] More broadly, they also point out that what works in fostering cognitive skills, such as problem solving, aligns well with best practices in developing social and emotional skills.

Even in this very hands-on environment, however, teachers maintain a crucial role by facilitating student learning. The psychologist Richard Mayer, an expert in the learning sciences and their application in education, has conducted and reviewed many studies that compare the outcomes of students learning entirely on their own with teacher-facilitated learning. He consistently finds that children who have a teacher to guide their learning perform better in all areas, from problem solving to computer programming, showing that students need both enough freedom and "enough guidance so that their cognitive activity results in the construction of useful knowledge."[16] Teachers need to substantially complement lecture-focused teaching with pedagogical practices that characterize playful learning experiences.

As we move from a hop to a leap along the leapfrog pathway, learning is increasingly driven by student interest and need, and teachers increasingly assume the role of facilitator. Complementing the example of Brazil's NAVE is the Innova Schools network in Peru.[17] At this chain of low-cost private schools, blended learning (online and in-class learning) is the name of the game. Students spend 70 percent of the day in classrooms of 30 students; the other 30 percent is spent in a computer lab working at their own pace on individual learning plans. During the group instruction portion of the day, students work in small teams to tackle challenges related to curricular topics. When they move to the computer labs, students use online learning tools like Khan Academy and develop individual projects focused on their interests and learning needs, with teachers circulating throughout the labs to provide occasional support. Additionally, the school teaches design thinking to learners: once each year, students work in groups to apply their content knowledge to community social problems and to design human-centered innovations. Reaching 9,000 total learners, Innova Schools have promising evidence of success. On average, schools in the Innova network score 34 percentage points higher on mathematics and 38 on reading than national averages on Peru's government assessments.

Learning   In 1956, Benjamin Bloom developed a framework for student learning behaviors in order to promote higher forms of thinking in education. The revised version of this framework, known simply as Bloom's Taxonomy, describes a range of increasingly sophisticated learning objectives and behaviors. At its core, the taxonomy is about how learners interact with knowledge—how they think. It is a continuum that builds from the simple and concrete to the complex and abstract. As learners move from "lower-order" to "higher-order" skills, they are able to accomplish increasingly sophisticated learning objectives.[18] This movement requires students to demonstrate increasing levels of agency in the learning process. Take, for example, a lesson on the fairy tale "Little Red Riding Hood." The first level of thinking might require learners to describe where Little Red Riding Hood was walking, remembering information from the book. The final level could ask learners to create a poem or song that conveys Little Red's story in a new way. We rely on this taxonomy to describe a shift in what we expect of students: moving from what they know to what they can do with what they know.

Several studies justify this focus on both knowledge and application. For example, in the OECD Education Working Paper "How Teachers Teach and Students Learn," researchers using the PISA study compared the mathematics abilities of students from around the world who rely on memorization with those who use higher-order cognitive strategies, including consciously connecting tasks with prior knowledge or planning and setting goals.[19] They find that, on the most basic math questions, students using memorization strategies perform similar to others. However, these students are much less likely to succeed at more complex questions.

Of course, higher-order cognitive skills not only build on lower-order ones but also help to strengthen them. In a recent review of dozens of studies on cognitive development and literacy, researchers underscore the fact that complex skills are deeply intertwined with lower-order skills. For readers and writers to thrive, they need to learn both the cognitive basics, such as decoding words, and higher-order skills, such as inference.[20] One study showed that training fourth-graders in making inferences helped improve learning outcomes for poor readers; researchers posited that these readers likely struggled because they lacked the higher-order ability to draw connections between ideas, not because they lacked basic word-decoding abilities.[21] The additive nature of our leapfrog pathway reflects this awareness of skills interdependence, in which the creative capacities of learners are supported by their ability to remember and understand knowledge.

This support structure is equally relevant in the context of 21st-century skills, which can be developed by allowing students the opportunity to utilize diverse skills while learning specific academic content.[22] For example, students could hone their ability to collaborate with others in science class by working in teams to investigate the habitats of different animals. Integrating the development of 21st-century skills into traditional classroom subjects—teaching "skills through subjects"—is an important strategy for cultivating the breadth of skills.

As we move along the leapfrog pathway, education increasingly requires learners to create and evaluate original work using a broad range of skills, from academic to interpersonal and intrapersonal. A "skip" along the pathway's learning dimension might include Preparation for Social Action, a Ugandan tutorial-based program for in- and out-of-school youth in rural areas that teaches learners to apply math, science, technology, and language concepts to community development activities in agriculture, health, early childhood development, and environmental sustainability. Trained community tutors facilitate three-hour learning sessions five times per week that unite academic learning with social action. Though students are not transforming or creating knowledge themselves, they do apply classroom knowledge to real-world contexts. For example, they might use math concepts to analyze a local business's cash flow, or learn biology by studying local agricultural activities. In contrast, the start of this pathway dimension is characterized by the U.S.-based innovation Algebrator, a for-fee software program that helps students solve and understand high school– and college-level math problems. Students input problems from their textbooks or classroom notes into Algebrator, and the platform shows step-by-step instructions on how to solve it.

### *Recognition of Learning: Increasingly Individualized*

Shaun Webber was trying to do good. Like many of his contemporaries in South African human resources departments, Shaun spent the years immediately after apartheid trying to incorporate black professionals into his construction company. But, upon beginning his recruitment efforts, he noticed a problem. No matter where he looked, he simply could not find enough qualified candidates. He set out to investigate the talent pipeline, and soon a leak became clear: secondary education. Despite their interest in construction-related fields from civil engineering to safety management, too many students of color were simply unequipped to pursue such careers because they had had limited learning opportunities in science and mathematics. Discussions with friends at the Western Cape Education Department in Cape Town confirmed his suspicions and spurred him to dream up a new model for supporting diverse learners to become well-rounded professionals.

Since 1999, Go for Gold has served disadvantaged youth in the Western Cape through its four-phase program. It begins in high school, when students complete after-school coursework in math, science, technology, and life skills. Participants are recruited based on community need and student interest and are held to high standards. To join the program, students submit a personal statement and complete multiple rounds of panel interviews; to remain in Go for Gold, they must adhere to strict attendance and engagement criteria in their first year. To foster the professional competencies that employers demand, Go for Gold's extracurricular coursework focuses on skills such as communication, self-management, cognitive skills, and relationship building. Throughout the year, students have the chance to learn about careers in the construction industry by participating in career fairs, holiday camps, company visits, and mentorship programs led by industry professionals and Go for Gold alumni.

Near the end of phase one, students interview with partner companies to secure a yearlong work placement. In the second phase—a preuniversity gap year—students continue their math, science, and life skills coursework while interning at participating companies. Paid the same wage as an entry-level worker, students have the opportunity to rotate though and observe different departments within the company during their gap year and receive leadership development support through Go for Gold.

Bridging coursework prepares students for phase three: tertiary education. With the support of their host companies, students complete postsecondary training in a chosen field within the built environment and technical studies disciplines. Having seen the students in action during phase two, most companies opt to sponsor their trainees through their tertiary studies. For students whose companies are unable to sponsor their degree, Go for Gold offers its own scholarship fund and assistance in applying to external scholarships with references from Go for Gold and the student's host company.

Graduation marks phase four, when students secure full-time employment in the construction industry, usually at their host companies. The final phase of the Go for Gold program sees students with a job in hand, and partner companies benefit from a diverse talent pool they have trained themselves. Graduating students rarely leave the Go for Gold family; they give back by mentoring younger participants and participating in the professional alumni network.

Go for Gold stands as a unique model of authentically verifying learning. Instead of simply choosing candidates based on credentials such as postsecondary degrees—rough proxies for student skills and competencies at best—employers are able to evaluate learners directly in their future workplaces. After a year of work experience and mentorship, employers are intimately familiar with candidates' work. For example, Bongani, an aspiring civil engineer, demonstrated both his empathy and technical expertise by completing a bridge design for a sick colleague without being asked. In another example, Jessica proved she was a skilled orator by presenting a large construction contract to a government agency and winning the bid for her team. Moreover, employers have a hand in shaping these competencies before hiring; students benefit from real-time feedback and targeted development through Go for Gold's mentorship schemes and co-designed life skills and leadership classes. More than 80 percent of Go for Gold's 600 participants achieved a bachelor's pass on the secondary leaving exam—the score required to attend college. This stands in stark contrast to the 27 percent of South African youth who obtain such a result nationally. More promising yet, 80 percent of participants completed tertiary studies on time, and all secured full-time employment following graduation.[23]

How learning is recognized often frames how teachers teach inside their classrooms, what schools measure, and how institutions such as employers and universities select which young people to accept. Consequently, any attempt to leapfrog teaching and learning practices needs to go hand in hand with shifting practices in how to assess and certify learning. Two elements of recognizing student learning focus on authentically aligning student classroom experiences with their practical, real-world contexts.

Although most employers intend to hire employees based on what they can do, to date most have relied on proxy measures of candidates' competencies—namely, degrees and diplomas. Students' progress in school often is based on how long they spend in their classes, combined with whether they meet at least a minimum level of content mastery. In the end, they are awarded a diploma that signifies the time they spent learning and, to some extent, the knowledge they acquired. However, this certification rarely captures the full range of their competencies. New models for recognizing student learning are emerging today, such as expanding the types of skills and abilities against which teachers track student growth, allowing for progression once a skill is developed, and demonstrating competence directly to employers—in other words, approaches that increasingly recognize individual differences in students' learning and skills (figure 5-3).

**Progression**   In most learning environments, students are grouped into age grades where they learn together and at the same pace. There is a linear progression from one grade to the next, and students move together through their classes and onto the next grade. This approach frequently uses assessments to determine whether a student can move to the next age grade; for example, students may be required to repeat a grade if they do not achieve passing marks in their courses. However, this system largely treats age as one of the most important determinants of student ability. By providing limited flexibility in how we recognize learners' abilities,

**FIGURE 5-3** Recognition of Learning: Increasingly Individualized

## PROGRESSION

POTENTIAL TO
LEAPFROG

## VERIFICATION

Education-led +
Hybrid-led +

Predetermined +
Group-based +

**INDUSTRY-LED:**
Employers and postsecondary
institutions mediate the
verification process.
Employers and postsecondary
institutions find ways to
directly recognize learners'
knowledge and skills that are
of particular relevance to their
job or further course of study.

**INDIVIDUAL-BASED:**
Learners progress individually
as they demonstrate mastery
of content. They move fluidly
between learning groups and
may have the option of
designing their own
assessments and pathways.

LEAP

Education-led +

**HYBRID-LED:**
Educational institutions
mediate the verification
process, in collaboration with
employers and postsecondary
institutions. Employers and
postsecondary institutions
recognize diplomas and other
certifications with the
knowledge that they have
contributed to students'
educational programming in
some capacity.

Predetermined +

**GROUP-BASED:**
Learners progress based on
ability, to a limited extent.
They can sometimes move
between groups of similarly-
leveled peers.

SKIP

**EDUCATION-LED:**
Educational institutions
mediate the verification
process. Employers and
postsecondary institutions
recognize diplomas and other
certifications from formal
institutions.

**PREDETERMINED:**
Learners progress based on
time and age in a linear
fashion.

HOP

we erase individual difference between learners—both struggles and strengths.

Research from learning sciences consistently shows that one of the most impactful teaching practices is the continuous assessment of student ability in order to tailor academic content appropriately.[24] Teaching that matches student needs is equally important for fostering social and emotional skills.[25] Proponents of ability-based progression often talk about the widely examined pedagogical approaches of "mastery-based learning" or "competency-based" learning.[26] These efforts provide differentiated supports to ensure that learners master needed skills, developing novel assessments that can capture this mastery in not only academic but also interpersonal and intrapersonal skills, and devising progression mechanisms that give students the time needed to master a skill.[27] Useful assessment practices that can help more authentically reflect students' competencies include self-assessments and peer assessments, computerized adaptive quizzes, and student portfolios. Preliminary evidence suggests that such approaches, which focus on what learners can do with their knowledge, lead to improved learning outcomes.[28]

As we advance along our leapfrog pathway, programming increasingly allows learners to progress based on individual knowledge and need. A prime example of the individualized, mastery-based progression at the end of the pathway is Australia's Alberton Primary School. Through its "Discovery" program, students collaborate on personal learning plans that allow them to determine what and how they want to learn. They identify topics of interest and propose learning projects to complete individually or in groups, where older learners develop leadership and empathy skills by mentoring younger learners with similar interests. As students' needs and interests evolve, they can design new learning pathways, identify new learning goals, and move between diverse interest and ability groups. Alberton serves 290 learners yearly, and its students consistently receive above-average results on state and national standardized tests.

**Verification**    However, it will not be sufficient to change how learning is recognized within the formal education system alone. At the end of the day, we seek to equip youth with the skills they need to thrive outside schools. In considering how to determine when students have learned what they need to know, our attention necessarily turns to employers and post-secondary institutions—those who ultimately must determine whether youth are prepared for what comes after school. Currently, employers rely on the skills information they can glean from diplomas and credentials, accredited by formal systems of education, which may indicate some of the skills that graduates have but rarely showcase all the skills that an employer desires. Likewise, many universities depend on standardized test scores and grades, which illuminate only a small part of what students can do. In the end, educational qualifications act as a proxy measure for individual skills, painting a broad picture of what students should be able to do for employers and postsecondary institutions.

External actors have experimented with ways to recognize and verify students' learning, particularly through tools that will allow institutions and employers to verify the specific competencies they seek. These tools include badges, which are digital "representations of skills" that are issued and shared by organizations and individuals, and physical or digital portfolios that showcase student creations.[29] Other approaches use formal linkages with employers and postsecondary institutions to give them a voice in what students learn and how they are assessed. Through these connections with individual educational programs, employers and post-secondary institutions can screen candidates with greater confidence in the specific skills their diplomas represent.

A focus on competency is not a novel concept. In the arts, for example, the world's top ballerina would not be barred from auditioning for the Royal Ballet in London if she did not have a degree in dance; nor do great painters need a master's degree in fine arts before they can be exhibited in top museums. Technology industries have begun to use this approach as well; whereas one would usually need a computer science degree to demonstrate that he or she has the skills required for a coding job, code storage platforms like GitHub and badge-enabled coding games like CodeFights allow learners to directly demonstrate their skills to employers. Both sectors indicate what education will have to emulate across the board: systems in which education institutions no longer serve as proxies for the labor market or postsecondary education. This ultimately opens up multiple pathways for students to demonstrate their individual abilities.

As we advance along our leapfrog pathway, educational programming increasingly forms partnerships with actors from outside the formal system to determine if students have particular skills and abilities. An intermediate step on this path is to allow employers or postsecondary institutions to provide some input on the skills and competencies that schools teach and assess. Take, for example, the case of the School-Business Partnerships program by Al Jisir and INJAZ Al-Maghrib in Morocco. Dreamed up by a former banker, the program links private sector companies with individual schools to improve the quality and relevance of Moroccan education. Companies are invited to "adopt" schools, providing both financial and technical support through School Support Committees composed of business leaders, administrators, teachers, students, and parents. These committees conduct collaborative, in-school needs assessments and develop three-year action plans for school improvement. Business leaders lend their strategic and managerial expertise to school administrators, fund school improvement projects, participate in classroom and extracurricular activities, and offer advice on incorporating business skills into the curricula at the national, municipal, and school levels. Additionally, through INJAZ Al-Maghrib, businesspeople advise students as they develop and pilot small businesses and facilitate workshops on entrepreneurship, financial literacy, and life skills. Students at these schools receive a regular diploma accredited by the Moroccan government, but they study a curriculum developed in collaboration with employers. The program has served more than 150,000 students across 300 public schools.

### Support Elements: Increasingly Diverse and Results-Oriented

Support elements assist the core elements in transforming what and how children learn. These elements leverage more people and places and the power offered by technology and data. They are not necessary for educational transformation but often are helpful, especially when considering the scale of educational challenges. For example, an innovation can support transformed teaching and learning through technology without leveraging more people—in addition to teachers—to assist in the learning process.

*People and Places: Increasingly Diverse*

Like all good things, it began with a game. Javier González Quintero, a young teacher fresh out of college, sat at a battered plastic table on a concrete patio overlooking the Colombian countryside. Against a cloudless blue sky, green mountains flecked with the vibrant reds and purples of old-growth coffee trees cut the horizon. Around the plastic table sat the family members of one of his best students—a trio of men, broad-shouldered and bronzed from long days tending to coffee trees in the harsh summer sun. Javier had made the winding trek up to visit this family's farm after receiving little feedback on the report cards he had his students bring home. Probing his students for details, he confirmed his suspicions: the vast majority of adults in the community could neither read nor write; his report cards were useless.

So he went to relate his student reports in person. When he arrived at the first family's home, the men of the house quickly invited him to play a game of dominoes. They played the game with a cunning and talent against which Javier could not hope to win, laying each piece with such artful strategy that he had lost within minutes of the game's start. And, at the end of the match, they tallied their points before Javier was halfway through compiling his own score.

In that moment, it hit him. These adults had all of the cognitive skills needed to master reading: the logical memory, the sharp focus, the mental agility. What if they could learn to read the same way they had learned dominoes—through play?

And so the abcdespañol game was born. What began as an intervention designed to teach illiterate adults quickly grew to serve early-grade learners in Colombia, the Dominican Republic, India, and beyond. Instead of the middle-aged farmers crowded around a domino table, LEMA, the Literacy Education and Math Lab, now works with bright-eyed 6- to 10-year-olds, huddled around small boxes containing sets of plastic, domino-like chips.

The idea is simple: in one of LEMA's literacy games, learners pick up a chip, labeled with a word like "dog" and a corresponding picture, and place it on a matching square. Teams of learners race to match words and pictures, challenging each other to develop rules for why a given letter pairing matches its corresponding image. The game then increases in complexity, pushing learners to explore, discover, and develop hypotheses. At its core, LEMA is about teaching language systems—including the language of mathematics—through exploration, collaboration, and risk taking.

After identifying language rules, patterns, and quirks through this game-based group work, learners have time to record their findings in individual workbooks. The result is that students acquire a deep understanding of language systems and, of equal importance, develop core interpersonal and cognitive skills like collaboration, critical thinking, and oral fluency, all of which are necessary for success in learning and life. To complement its literacy interventions, LEMA has come to develop games that foster learners' foundational knowledge of such topics as fractions and complex grammar.

Key to the LEMA model is its flexibility with regard to where learning takes place and who supports students on their learning journeys. In the Dominican Republic, for example, LEMA sessions were a part of the regular school day. There, public school teachers received support from trained volunteers, known as Learning Coaches (LCs), who entered classrooms to facilitate small-group LEMA learning sessions. In India, schoolteachers participated in 20 hours of professional development, empowering them to integrate playful learning into their literacy and math classes. Meanwhile, in Colombia, LEMA sessions are facilitated entirely by LCs—often local mothers—and take place after school in empty community buildings.

In all contexts, however, the community takes center stage. Though LCs come from diverse walks of life—including parents, former teachers, and even literate older siblings—the recruitment process is rigorous. "The most important criteria for LC selection," notes Catalina González, director of LEMA's parent organization, Literacy4All, "is curiosity: we want facilitators who see themselves as learners, and can impart their love of learning to the students they serve." Before working with learners, LCs complete a host of trainings on developmental theory and early grade pedagogy. Most important, however, Literacy4All organizes these trainings to model the type of playful pedagogy that LCs will support through LEMA; any given training session might find LCs participating in dance classes, learning yoga, or making their own board games.

Besides allowing Literacy4All to affordably expand and scale LEMA labs, incorporating a diverse set of people and places into programming fosters relevant learning experiences that are responsive to local contexts. Having studied in the same cultural environments as the students they serve, LCs stand as academic role models and show that learning is indeed possible. Additionally, given their cultural knowledge, they are uniquely equipped to engage learners authentically.

Perhaps the local economy depends on coffee; in such a context, an LC might tap her cultural expertise to adapt LEMA games to teach literacy using farm vocabulary. Or take the case of El Salado, a small town in Colombia's northern mountain range and the site of a notorious massacre of civilians by paramilitary forces in 2000. Schoolteachers who were bused in from neighboring villages to alleviate teacher shortages approached the community with fear, rushing to leave town each afternoon, but LCs from the local community stood with learners in solidarity. Literacy outcomes soared as students learned alongside adults who understood and openly addressed the burden they collectively carried.

Over its 35-year history, LEMA has served nearly one million learners across four continents. LEMA programming currently benefits more than 3,000 students in Colombia, Guatemala, Panama, India, and the United States. Though data collection efforts differ considerably between program sites, impact studies in the Dominican Republic and Panama suggest that LEMA can develop basic literacy skills in as little as 90 hours of play. For example, over the course of one year, first-grade LEMA students in the Dominican Republic improved their scores on a literacy assessment by 50 percentage points, surpassing third-graders' average beginning-of-year scores by 15 percentage points. Even more exciting than these assessment gains, however, is the anecdotal evidence that participants provide on students' 21st-century skill growth. As one Colombian teacher notes, "LEMA is about so much more than literacy. Children often begin without knowing the sound of the letter 'a,' and they certainly learn that in our sessions. But, more important, they leave LEMA confident, collaborative critical thinkers."[30]

Throughout history, education has always taken place in diverse contexts: within the home, in artisans' workshops, and inside places of worship, to name a few. Children regularly rely on a wide array of people to prepare them with the skills they needed. Older siblings pass down knowledge, parents contribute their expertise, community members work with youth to solve community problems, and local businesses provide hands-on learning opportunities related to their industries. Education has intentionally utilized diverse contexts that include schools and online communities, but also community spaces, workplaces, and the natural environment. In a world facing teacher shortages alongside a growing youth population, everyone will need to come together to address these twin problems. Although it may not be necessary to leverage more people and places in order to transform what and how children learn, the scale of our problems is so vast that leapfrogging will draw heavily on these supports (figure 5-4).

**People**    Successful leapfrogging in teaching, learning, and recognition depends a great deal on helping to unburden teachers and unleash their creativity. Arguments against tackling skills inequality and skills uncertainty together often include the feasibility of asking overwhelmed educators and school personnel to make large changes to their approaches and curricula. This is certainly a valid concern, given that teachers in almost every country face a long list of responsibilities, from administrative duties to assisting with schoolwide functions, that have little to do with meaningful learning in their classrooms.[31] In one extreme example, the Pakistani government requires teachers to spend approximately 50 days per year on nonteaching duties, such as staffing vaccination drives and voting centers.[32] It is unsurprising, then, that the CUE report *Millions Learning: Scaling Up Quality Education in Developing Countries* found unburdening and empowering teachers to be one of the key ingredients of successfully scaling up effective approaches to improving learning.[33]

For this reason, leapfrogging will require us to consider new ways to unburden teachers. Reinforcing this idea, the Education Commission used the example of Chile to point out that teachers have an average of less than half a person supporting them in their work, compared with the five medical personnel supporting doctors.[34] Indeed, with its community health worker approach, the global health community provides a prime example of the power of tapping diverse groups of people. Community health workers are community members who have been trained to take on

**FIGURE 5-4** People and Places: Increasingly Diverse

**PEOPLE**

POTENTIAL TO
LEAPFROG

**PLACES**

In-school +
Connected to outside school +

Licensed teachers +
Teachers team with others +

**IN A DIVERSITY OF CONTEXTS:**
Formal, organized learning significantly uses multiple spaces, including schools, community spaces, and workplaces. In some cases, these may be informal learning spaces where the environments are transformed for learning.

**EVERYONE:**
Learning regularly involves community members, peers, parents, siblings, employers, and others, along with educators.

**LEAP**

Licensed teachers +

In-school +

**TEACHERS TEAM WITH OTHERS:**
Licensed teachers sometimes team with parents, students, and others.

**SKIP**

**CONNECTED TO OUTSIDE SCHOOL:**
Learning is primarily organized in a formal setting but may sometimes occur outside the school building and hours—online or in person.

**LICENSED TEACHERS:**
Licensed teachers bear the entire responsibility of teaching.

**HOP**

**IN-SCHOOL:**
Learning is formal, organized, and occurs inside a defined space and time (school day).

various tasks previously carried out by physicians, such as administering vaccines or providing prenatal support. Supervised by a medical expert, the health workers leverage their community knowledge and geographical flexibility to unburden doctors and scale up effective medical interventions—in effect, bringing the clinic to the people rather than the people to the clinic.[35] Our pathway illustrates a similar effort in education to unburden teachers, bolster the education workforce, and ultimately facilitate leapfrogging.

Educational programming increasingly leverages nonteacher actors to help unburden teachers and support learning. Aflatoun, a financial and social education program developed by the Dutch nongovernment organization (NGO) Aflatoun International, represents a skip along this dimension. It offers highly flexible curricula for preschool to teenaged learners, usually in formal education settings. Community partners adapt the curricula, which focus on children's rights, money management, and enterprise, to local contexts. Aflatoun trains local teachers to deliver these curricula in formal settings, using active learning methodologies to develop youth skills for employability and entrepreneurship, including teamwork, creativity, and citizenship. Central to the Aflatoun model is the development of "children's clubs," which focus on peer-to-peer collaboration, problem solving, and democratic leadership. Through these clubs, students teach and learn from each other as they start small businesses and lead community development projects. More than 4.5 million learners benefit from Aflatoun programming annually, and randomized controlled trial evidence found that the program's positive effect on financial habits was more than double that of the 25 other financial education interventions studied.

Camfed's Learner Guide Program complements LEMA to demonstrate a leap along the people dimension of the pathway. The program trains young women who have participated in Camfed programming to serve as mentors and peer teachers in rural African schools. These women, known as Learner Guides, deliver a curriculum on self-awareness, resilience, discernment, and well-being. They also provide tutoring and informal mentorship support to local learners. Upon completion of the program, Learner Guides receive access to low-risk, interest-free loans and qualify for fast-track teacher certifications. So far, 4,660 Learner Guides have served more than 250,000 students. An independent evaluation found that 91 percent of students surveyed reported that the Learner Guide program positively affected their attitude toward school. Additionally, academic outcomes in Learner Guide schools improved by the equivalent of 0.5 effect size in English and 1.0 in mathematics.

**Places**     Classrooms are by no means the only place where children can develop the broad range of skills they need to thrive. The OECD, in its detailed 2013 report *Innovative Learning Environments*, argues that "'school' and 'classroom' do not offer a satisfactory architecture for framing learning environments as they are essentially institutional and partial."[36] Instead, they prefer the concept of the "learning environment" to illuminate the types of educational approaches that systems should use to effectively prepare students for the 21st century. A learning environment can draw on experiences both in and out of school, with a range of content and people from whom to learn. In their analysis, the pedagogical core of a learning environment has four main components: learners; content; educators, from licensed teachers to others; and resources, from learning spaces such as buildings to digital resources. Organized learning is carried out depending on the dynamics within that core, from how time is used to how learners and teachers are grouped to what pedagogy used.[37]

The term "life-wide" learning expresses the idea of seamlessly finding ways for children to learn important skills both in and out of school. The literature on this concept emphasizes the small proportion of waking hours that children typically spend inside school. For example, in the United States, from birth to age 18, children spend 20 percent of their waking hours in school.[38] The OECD's Center for Educational Research and Innovation defines life-wide learning as learning that takes place "in multiple contexts, such as work, at home and in our social lives."[39] Proponents of life-wide learning use this information to argue that there are many opportunities to creatively and thoughtfully expand the spaces in which children can learn. Being open to new people and places for learning is one important way to quickly enrich young people's learning experiences that develop skills for the future.

Substantial evidence demonstrates the ways in which leveraging diverse settings to offer various extracurricular activities can help children learn, with special promise for interpersonal and intrapersonal skills. In 2016, University College London's Centre for Longitudinal Studies published a paper highlighting the strong association between participation in activities outside of school and positive outcomes in both school attainment and social and emotional skills development for rich and disadvantaged youth alike.[40] The study emphasized the skills-building potential of activities occurring beyond school walls—both formal activities, such as music lessons in community centers, and informal activities, such as playing sports in a park. A 2013 study from the German Socio-Economic Panel provides evidence that, controlling for family variables, music training outside of school improves cognitive and noncognitive skills development and leads to higher performance in and engagement with school.[41] Analyses of nonformal education in the developing world have yielded similarly positive results; in Nicaragua, for example, researchers have shown that participation in academic programming outside of schools leads to higher learning outcomes and greater civic and social engagement.[42]

There is increasing interest in finding scalable ways in which children can learn academic and interpersonal and intrapersonal skills outside the classroom, a push driven largely by recent technological advancements. Such approaches include everything from the tens of millions of people around the world taking open courses on Khan Academy or Ed-X to Sudan's tablet-based Can't Wait to Learn program. Using new applications of augmented reality, the same software that powers the Pokémon Go mobile phone game can turn any environment into an educational experience in which students can explore and learn from their surroundings.[43] But out-of-school learning is not limited to technology-enabled environments. For example, Kathy Hirsh-Pasek, a CUE colleague and a professor of learning science at Temple University, has designed physical spaces in supermarkets that boost children's language acquisition dramatically.[44] Her team has expanded this work and, together with partners in the U.S. city of Philadelphia, is transforming bus stops, street corners, and abandoned lots into places of learning.[45] Benches that double as puzzles, irregular hop-scotches, and lamp designs that reveal different shapes when moved are all ways that Hirsh-Pasek is testing whether the science of learning can help shape urban design and planning in a way that lets young people hone their critical thinking, problem solving, and literacy and numeracy skills through play.[46] Ultimately, she hopes to transform cities into learning landscapes.

As we advance along the leapfrog pathway, educational programming increasingly leverages the potential of nonformal learning spaces to supplement classroom instruction. At the end of this pathway, we would find an innovation like Peads. This NGO operates in formal and nonformal education programs in rural Brazil to make learning more applicable to students and families in agricultural areas. Peads links classroom work with rural development needs by facilitating student-led research on issues related to agriculture, including innovative farming techniques and agricultural technology. Students venture into their communities both during and after school to identify community needs and develop community-based projects that put academic skills into practice in local contexts. For example, students might research soil erosion on coffee farms, analyze the impact it has on coffee production, develop a plan to train farmers on soil conservation, and then evaluate the success of their intervention. Peads has reached over 130,000 learners across Brazil and won fifth place in the Itaú UNICEF Education and Participation Awards, one of the highest distinctions for NGOs in Brazil.

### Technology and Data: Increasingly Results-Oriented

Today, Poonam is a racecar driver. Winding along tree-lined streets, she deftly dodges a floating white bubble labeled "59," swerving to collect the number "28." Though she spent the school day completing multiplication worksheets alongside her Class III peers, it is back to basics here at the after-school Mindspark Center. Yesterday's racetrack was peppered with advanced multiplication facts, but today's tasks her with identifying multiples of two on a highway full of distractions. The switch comes not because Poonam had incorrectly navigated yesterday's race—in fact, she scored highest among her peers—but rather because she struggled to fold a square into eighths during the subsequent virtual origami activity.

Without formal testing, and without even alerting Poonam to the change, Mindspark—the adaptive learning platform on which she plays after school—notes that she has simply memorized her multiplication tables. She does not understand the mathematical process underpinning such calculations. Immediately, it reroutes her math journey and constructs an opportunity to build understanding of fundamentals factor rules.

This is the beauty of adaptive learning technologies. All around Poonam, in an unadorned room filled with dozens of computers, headphone-clad Indian schoolchildren clatter away on their keyboards. Some Class III students practice one-digit addition by counting repeating shapes in art deco paintings, as others build mazes using budding geometric knowledge; still others take a break from math entirely to read about cricket competitions or space travel, with story vocabulary that automatically changes to allow for comfortable exploration. No matter where their Mindspark adventures take them, all of these students are learning at the speed that is right for them and having fun while they do it.

In schools, teachers use Mindspark to enrich their teaching and differentiate instruction to serve heterogeneous classrooms. A comprehensive dashboard allows instructors to monitor students' work in real time, customize learning topics and progressions, and even identify the exact misconceptions that drive students' incorrect answers. Parents, too, can use the platform to access visual and narrative summaries of their children's accomplishments and struggles. In India today, the technology is used in 70 public schools in the low-income state of Rajasthan, serving over 12,000 students, and in over 150 private school classrooms. It has even made its way into a handful of American institutions.

Grounded in a host of academic literature on what works in teaching and learning, Mindspark has shown promising results. For example, in a randomized control trial study by the Abdul Latif Jameel Poverty Action Lab (J-PAL), researchers found that students who attended Mindspark Centers over four-and-a-half months improved their math and Hindi scores by 0.36 and 0.22 standard deviations respectively. In practical terms, this means that Mindspark students grew their test scores more than twice as fast as students who did not participate. Particularly heartening is the observation that Mindspark's adaptive learning experiences most benefited students who were struggling in school. All of this learning can be achieved at scale for under two dollars per month—less than 10 percent of the monthly per-pupil spending in Delhi's public schools.[47]

Technology and data are both important tools that can help education leapfrog to a breadth of skills for all learners. In both cases, however, more is not necessarily the answer. The potential of technology and data to support new learning experiences has grown in recent years, with features such as real-time student feedback or augmented reality beginning to enter the mainstream. Yet both have also suffered from a legacy of getting in the way of intended outcomes rather than unleashing the potential of students, educators, and community members to achieve desired results. Technology and data alone may not be required to transform what and how children learn. However, given the scope of our educational challenge, both can provide powerful supports if deployed in meaningful ways (figure 5-5).

**Technology**   One well-known framework for understanding how to use technology effectively in education is the SAMR model, developed by Ruben R. Puentedura in 2006.[48] As a graduate student at Harvard University in the 1980s, working to redesign the undergraduate science curriculum, Puentedura began to reflect on the role of technology in education transformation.[49] His research seeking to understand whether technology practices or tools themselves mattered more for learning eventually led to the creation of SAMR, now widely used by education practitioners. The SAMR model focuses on four types of technology use in education: substitution, augmentation, modification, and redefinition.

The first two types of technology use, Puentedura argues, enhance the education being provided. In the first type, technology simply substitutes for the function of some other technology without changing what is fundamentally possible—for example, having students fill in digital versions of traditional worksheets. In the second type of use, technology is better integrated, augmenting a function. This might mean using automatically graded online worksheets, freeing up teachers' time.

Puentedura argues that the second two types of use are fundamentally different: they move beyond tweaking the current educational model to enable educational transformation. For example, the third type of use, modification, could mean students using geographic information system mapping technology to transform and display census data in a social studies class. The final type of use is redefinition, where technology can do

FIGURE 5-5   Technology and Data: Increasingly Results Oriented

**TECHNOLOGY**        POTENTIAL TO LEAPFROG        **DATA**

Data for compliance +
Data for program
improvement +

Substitution +
Augmentation +

**DATA FOR
TRANSFORMING
LEARNING EXPERIENCES:**
Collection and analysis of data
in real time; data are used to
evolve programs, increase
transparency, and/or improve
educational experiences and
outcomes; data are less
compliance-oriented and may
be less standardized.

**MODIFICATION AND
REDEFINITION:**
Technology allows for
significant task redesign or for
the creation of new tasks that
were previously inconceivable.
Technology is integrated and
embedded into learning.

**LEAP**

Data for compliance +

Substitution +

**DATA FOR PROGRAM
IMPROVEMENT:**
Infrequent collection and
analysis of data. Data may be
used to improve programming;
limited use of data for
improving learner outcomes.

**AUGMENTATION:**
Technology acts as a direct
tool substitute, with functional
improvement.

**SKIP**

**SUBSTITUTION:**
Technology acts as a direct
tool substitute, with no
functional change.

**HOP**

**DATA FOR COMPLIANCE:**
Infrequent collection and
analysis of data. Data are used
for routine compliance.

something previously inconceivable, such as expanding access to educational opportunities, amplifying active learning, and allowing teachers and students to create and innovate beyond the existing material.

A number of recent studies of education technology highlight the importance of technology in transforming learning; unfortunately, this finding does not reflect much of the impact of digital technologies on education to date.[50] Education and technology expert Michael Trucano argues that far too frequently, the approach to ICT in education has been to "dump hardware in schools [and] hope for magic to happen."[51] In a detailed review of digital education technology in Latin America, he argues that although the rhetoric focuses on technology doing something that previously was inconceivable, "in actual practice technology has largely been used to support traditional teaching and learning practices."[52]

Recent research has shown that, when technology is used to enable playful learning experiences, it is much more effective in improving learning outcomes—especially for marginalized children. In a review of studies looking at technology for at-risk students in the United States, Linda Darling-Hammond and her colleagues found that technology generally is not used productively for disadvantaged students. For these students, the focus is on improving core academic knowledge, and programs use approaches in which students merely remember or understand content. Rather than the "drill-and-kill" computer exercises currently used, the authors find that technology is successful when it is interactive, includes real-time feedback, and allows students to creatively apply what they learned.[53] Other academics argue that new technologies such as virtual reality can empower even more playful learning activities—allowing for more sophisticated opportunities for application, collaboration, and creation.[54] Using technology in this way can help drive student learning experiences toward what is needed if we are to leapfrog education: applying, evaluating, and creating knowledge.

Educational programming increasingly uses technology to redefine and reimagine teaching and learning tasks. Before a leap like Mindspark comes a skip like MindTap, a for-fee learning management system used by teachers across the globe. MindTap helps teachers plan lessons with a repository of adjustable readings, assignments, interactive multimedia, and quizzes. Teachers can also use the platform to monitor their students with real-time analytics on engagement, achievement, and satisfaction. It augments classroom practices without redesigning existing tasks, allowing teachers to streamline assignments, organize class information, and identify topics that need additional instruction in order to address individual student needs. Internal reports indicate that MindTap can lead to increases in math (37 percent) and literacy (19 percent) achievement.

**Data** For data and evidence to support leapfrogging education, we need to move past a culture of collecting data without making it useful for improving systems, programs, and learning. Learners can flourish even when data are not collected, but without data it is hard to know whether they are flourishing or not. Ultimately it is best if programs continuously collect and apply data to drive student learning, evolve programming, and create transparent systems. To support leapfrogging, strategies that make data increasingly integrated, meaningful, and transparent—empowering rather than distracting stakeholders, as they focus on student learning— are important. The *Millions Learning* report has highlighted this dynamic in learning at scale. Examples of successfully scaled education initiatives invariably made use of continuous feedback loops, in which the data collected were then used to design, inform, and sustain programming.[55]

Digital technology has also influenced how we collect, analyze, and use data. Typically, education systems have collected data on school enrollment, expenditures, and other basic measures of inputs and outputs. More recently, education systems also have focused on measuring student learning to hold schools and systems accountable for ensuring that students master the basics.[56] However, most education data usually are not made public, are not disaggregated, and are not in a usable format.[57] The promise of data and evidence have been limited, as education has not yet made the shift from "data for compliance" to "data for learning."[58]

However, we are living amid what many have termed a "data revolution."[59] New technologies are allowing vast amounts of data to be collected on everything from miniscule changes in atmospheric pressure to an individual's dietary choices. Advanced analysis techniques can gauge public opinion as well as detect flu outbreaks.[60] The excitement around the potential for data to improve our lives and transform services has made its way to education, with many asking how we can better use data to track what is working and hold our systems accountable.

Data and evidence can provide valuable support to leapfrogging education, empowering politicians, parents, and educators with information to transform student experiences. But this entails more than simply ramping up data collection efforts. As the UNESCO Institute for Statistics reports, data collection is counterproductive to the goal of supporting learning when the process leaves educators feeling overburdened.[61] Social accountability scholars Jonathan Fox and Joy Aceron take this one step further, noting that data are not useful when they are collected and disseminated exclusively in an upward direction, never to be seen by the collectors again.[62] In additional papers, Fox showed that behavior change results only when data are explained or packaged so as to be understandable and actionable;[63] data collection and dissemination alone do not empower stakeholder action.[64] This concept of usability demands that interventions using data pay attention to form in addition to process, with a particular emphasis on data format, presentation, and comparability.[65]

In the vision of data and evidence set forth here, these processes create a self-driving machine that enables systems of all sizes to make decisions and continuously improve performance. The World Bank education specialist Husein Abdul-Hamid refers to this dynamic power of data to inform and transform systems as the "information cycle."[66] As we advance along the leapfrog pathway, educational programming increasingly integrates data to improve education experiences and outcomes. A leap along this pathway uses data to drive learning. Carnegie Mellon University's Open Learning Initiative (OLI) is an example of such a leap. OLI is an online learning course provision platform that can be used by students outside of formal education contexts or by teachers for blended learning (online and in-class learning).[67] OLI uses automatic tutoring, virtual laboratories, activity-embedded assessments, and continuous feedback to tailor content to meet student needs. As students complete learning activities, OLI collects real-time data to determine what material to present next, as well as offering personalized corrections, suggestions, or cues to the student. These data are continuously provided to the instructor and used to tailor teaching materials and alter teaching methodologies. More than

300,000 users have accessed OLI. Randomized controlled trials confirm that self-directed OLI courses are as effective as traditional courses. When students use OLI materials in blended learning, they learn the same content twice as fast as they would in traditional classrooms.[68]

## Enabling Environment for Leapfrogging

Ultimately, the leapfrog pathway sets out a vision of expanding options to transform what and how children learn. Naturally, it will look very different in different contexts. Although this pathway charts a course for forward-looking educators, certain elements will be more relevant than others depending on the situations that young people face. Across all contexts, however, the ability to leapfrog will be mediated by the enabling environment, including the economic, political, social, and cultural factors that shape a particular community or country.

Recent research on what enables the scaling of effective interventions that improve learning identified various elements of an enabling environment as influential.[69] One such element was the appetite for a particular educational approach, whether expressed by community members, parents, or the students themselves. Properly aligning the demand from education receivers or "consumers" with the supply of educational services can help roll out and expand interventions. Likewise, a government policy environment that allows for flexible adaptation of educational provision strategies was another important element for scaling.

The leapfrog pathway does not include an analysis of the enabling environment needed for rapid, nonlinear progress, as the four pathway elements are solely focused on dimensions of educational service provision. This is not because we think that the enabling environment is unimportant. Rather, given the time constraints on our analysis, we focused our efforts on the crucial elements contained in the pathway.

One thing that should be emphasized, however, is the role of government in advancing education along the leapfrog pathway. As stated earlier, leapfrogging will not be achieved if we intentionally or unintentionally undermine governments' commitment to ensuring that all children have a right to education. By adding an expanding set of options for how to approach education, governments can open up avenues for leaping ahead that otherwise might have been closed. Yet these expanded options should not be interpreted as a shift in the ultimate responsibility for educating all children. Governments ultimately must be responsible for providing mass education, where every child in society has the opportunity to learn. Mass education, after all, is a social project intended not only to help individual children develop to their full potential but also to advance broader aims across society. Currently, society is organized along the lines of nation-states; until another social system takes shape, governments are the only social actors that have the duty to care for and protect the rights of every young person—something that neither civil society nor the business community is currently bound to do.

*Six*

# The Potential to Leapfrog

## What We Learned about the Education Innovations Community

Where is the education innovation community focusing its energy? We have illustrated the boundaries of the leapfrog pathway with some examples of innovations. However, a collective examination of the innovations could provide insight into the scope and scale of the innovation efforts, the ways in which the education innovation community treats the elements of the leapfrog pathway, and the efforts themselves. Ultimately, this will illuminate how the education innovations community can contribute to leapfrogging.

We began our research by uniting 16 existing lists of education innovations to create a catalog of nearly 3,000 projects, programs, and schools. The lists came from Innovation Spotters—organizations that actively identify, highlight, and sometimes support education innovations around the world. Rather than being selective in our choices, we analyzed every intervention that these Spotters deemed innovative. Our only requirement was that the spotter organization explicitly stated that they were identifying what they believed to be innovations. Figure 6-1 provides an overview of the information that we collected on each innovation and table 6-1 profiles the 16 Spotters included in our catalog.

### Scope and Scale of Innovations

Innovations in the catalog address all ages and types of education, from early childhood development to higher education. However, because we focused on leapfrogging K–12 education, we did not include in our research Innovation Spotters that focused solely on higher education. Unsurprisingly, 81 percent of cataloged innovations target primary- or secondary-aged learners.[1] Primary-aged youth are the largest target group in our catalog, with 65 percent of innovations, but secondary-level learners are not far behind, as 55 percent of innovations reach youth in this age cohort. Though our primary concern was the potential to leapfrog K–12 education, some of our lists contained innovations at other education levels and also are included in our catalog. Our catalog contains similar shares of interventions in early childhood development (17%), technical and vocational education (13%), and higher education (12%). The vast majority of innovations, around 81 percent, aim to improve learners' skills. Most innovations focus on helping children, youth, and adults learn, whether they operate in or out of schools. Almost a third of the innovations (29%) aim to improve access to education, including helping improve enrollment, attendance, and retention. A surprisingly small percentage of the innovations, only 23 percent, aim to advance teachers' professional development and capacity through teacher training or other activities (figure 6-2).

The innovations range from tiny schools that have served only a dozen learners to massive online platforms like Duolingo, a foreign language–learning app with more than 150 million registered users. Roughly a third of cataloged innovations report data on the total number of learners served. Of these, more than three-quarters have reached at least 1,000 learners, and 30 percent (320 innovations) have served 50,000 or more.

One reason that many innovations appear to be small scale is that the Innovation Spotters have focused their efforts on relatively recent innovations. Three-quarters of the cataloged innovations were established from 1997 on and have taken root in the past 20 years. Within that group, half of the cataloged innovations were established within the recent decade, with

**FIGURE 6-1** Snapshot: Global Education Innovations Catalog

### 16 SOURCES
*Innovation Spotter organizations with active lists of education innovations in 2016 and early 2017*

### 166 COUNTRIES
*From across the developed and developing world*

### 4 LANGUAGES
*Searched for lists in English, Spanish, Mandarin, and Portuguese*

### 2,854 INNOVATIONS
*Including NGO projects, for-profit products, government initiatives, and schools*

### INFORMATION COLLECTED ON EACH INNOVATION

| | |
|---|---|
| Descriptors | Name of primary actor(s) and innovation \| Country/countries and region(s) \| Year established \| Innovation goal(s) \| Age(s)/schooling level(s) targeted \| Skill(s) or subject(s) targeted \| Population(s) targeted \| Source list(s) \| Whether currently active \| Website link |
| Implementation details | Type(s) of implementer \| Type(s) of funding \| Effectiveness data \| Scale \| Cost |
| Leapfrog pathway characteristics | Learning \| Teaching \| Progression \| Verification \| People \| Places \| Technology \| Data |

**TABLE 6-1** Innovation Spotters Cataloged

| Innovation Spotter | Number of innovations | Focus | Geography | Collaboration with Other Spotters |
|---|---|---|---|---|
| Ashoka Fellows[a] and Changemaker Schools | 881 | Supporting and highlighting social innovators working in education and schools that promote changemaker skills | Global | R4D, WISE, Harvard, OECD |
| R4D–CEI Program Database | 756 | Highlighting pro-poor innovations in developing countries | Low- and middle-income countries | Harvard, WISE, Ashoka, OECD, UNICEF |
| EdSurge Curriculum Products[b] | 518 | U.S.-based education technology organization that highlights EdTech products for teachers, parents, and school leaders | United States and global | InnoveEdu |
| WISE–ed.hub, awards, and prizes | 249 | Providing a platform to highlight innovations through the hub, funding proven models through awards and prizes | Global | R4D, InnoveEdu, Harvard, Ashoka |
| OECD Innovative Learning Environments | 127 | Studying and highlighting innovative school models from OECD member countries | OECD (high-income) countries | R4D, Harvard |
| Graduate XXI/IDB | 122 | Initiative to identify technology projects to improve education and graduation in Latin America | Latin America | |
| HundrED Finnish 100 | 100 | Highlighting and studying 100 innovations currently taking place in Finnish schools | Finland | Ashoka |
| InnoveEdu | 98 | Highlighting initiatives and classifying their approaches, including technology products and low-tech programs | Global | WISE, EdSurge |
| UNICEF–Innovation Fund and Mapping | 61 | Highlighting innovations through its mapping, and funding programs through its fund | Low- and middle-income countries | R4D |

| | | | | |
|---|---|---|---|---|
| Harvard Global Education Innovations Initiative | 56 | Identifying and highlighting best practices for 21st-century learning | Global | WISE, OECD, R4D, Teach for All |
| Teach for All–Alumni Incubator | 47 | Supporting alumni from the Teach for All partner countries to create and scale up innovations | Global | Harvard |
| mEducation Alliance[d] | 36 | Hosts the Mobiles for Education Alliance Symposium, highlighting promising tech solutions for improving learning outcomes in developing countries | Low- and middle-income countries | All Children Reading: Grand Challenge for Development |
| All Children Reading: Grand Challenge for Development[c] | 30 | Collaboration between USAID, WorldVision, and the Australian government to catalyze, identify, and support tech innovations for early grade reading in developing countries | Low- and middle-income countries | mEducation |
| Development Innovation Ventures[a] | 10 | Investing in innovations that solve challenges in developing countries | Low- and middle-income countries | |
| Humanitarian Education Accelerator | 8 | Financing, mentoring, and providing evaluation support to humanitarian innovators with the goal of scaling up effective education solutions for youth in emergencies | Education in emergencies | |
| Global Innovation Fund[a] | 2 | Investing in innovations that meet challenges in developing countries through grants | Low- and middle-income countries | |

a. These lists included innovations from other sectors. We cataloged only those entries relevant to education.

b. We chose to catalog only the curriculum products from EdSurge's larger index, which consists of over 2,300 products, so as not to dilute the contributions of other Innovation Spotters and also because of the time it would take to include all of the innovations in the EdSurge list.

c. We chose to catalog only the winners of the Round 2, Enabling Writers, Mobiles for Reading 2014-15, Technology to Support Education in Crisis and Conflict Settings, and Tracking and Tracing Books competitions, given the limits of publicly available information on other prize winners.

d. We chose to catalog only the innovations featured at the 2016 mEducation Alliance Symposium, given the limited information available on past years' innovators, as well as the 2016 symposium's focus on evidenced innovations.

**FIGURE 6-2**  Primary Goal of Innovations

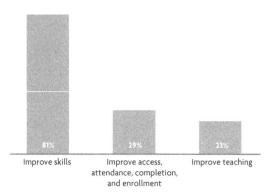

| | |
|---|---|
| 81% | |
| Improve skills | |
| 29% | |
| Improve access, attendance, completion, and enrollment | |
| 23% | |
| Improve teaching | |

a roughly even split between innovations less than 5 years old (25%) and those 5 to 10 years old (22%). Though innovations are most concentrated in the past decade, there is some variety in age. Eighteen percent of cataloged interventions are at least 20 years old; eight originated in the 19th century. These outliers are largely schools drawn from the Ashoka Schools or OECD lists. The oldest cataloged innovation, the Sidcot School in the United Kingdom, is an Ashoka Changemaker School and was founded in 1699. Despite this focus on new programming, the data reveal that the Spotters' criteria for scale in innovation are diverse; their focus is not limited to small pilots or to large-scale, established interventions.

*Strong Desire for Innovation in Rich and Poor Countries Alike*

One of the most striking features of the innovations in the catalog is their geographic diversity. With 166 countries represented, education innovation is clearly ongoing in poor and rich countries alike. There are 41 countries with 20 or more education innovations featured in the catalog, and they include some of the poorest countries in the world (Afghanistan and Nepal) as well as some of the wealthiest (Canada and Australia). The 15 countries with 50 or more innovations also have a mix of economic development levels, from Uganda to Finland. The two countries with the most innovations are India and the United States (figure 6-3).

**FIGURE 6-3** Where Are Innovations Occurring?

■ Countries with over 100 innovations     ▨ Countries with 1–19 innovations
▨ Countries with 20–99 innovations     ▨ Countries with 0 innovations

## Countries with 20+ Innovations

| | | | | | |
|---|---|---|---|---|---|
| 618 | United States | 51 | Australia | 27 | Nepal |
| 320 | India | 49 | Tanzania | 26 | Jordan |
| 187 | South Africa | 46 | Rwanda | 26 | Austria |
| 167 | Kenya | 46 | Argentina | 25 | Turkey |
| 130 | Brazil | 45 | Ghana | 24 | Ireland |
| 120 | Finland | 42 | China | 24 | Ethiopia |
| 94 | Uganda | 38 | Thailand | 24 | Egypt |
| 88 | Mexico | 38 | Peru | 22 | Senegal |
| 80 | United Kingdom | 38 | Indonesia | 22 | Afghanistan |
| 74 | Nigeria | 38 | Germany | 21 | Zimbabwe |
| 66 | Colombia | 37 | Spain | 20 | Uruguay |
| 65 | Canada | 36 | Bangladesh | 20 | Guatemala |
| 57 | Pakistan | 34 | France | 20 | Cambodia |
| 55 | Chile | 27 | Zambia | | |

The nations that appear most frequently in our catalog highlight a Spotter focus on large countries with widespread inequality in education and other contexts. But their appearance also stems in part from the geographical biases of some of our sources. For example, 76 percent of EdSurge's 518-item curriculum and product index is U.S.-based. R4D's Center for Education Innovations, whose database accounts for 26 percent of our catalog, collaborated extensively with regional hubs in India, South Africa, Kenya, and Uganda. Despite this relative overrepresentation, however, our Innovation Spotters still have a sweeping geographic reach.

Education innovators are searching for better approaches not only across poor and rich countries but also across those with strong and weak education systems. Of the countries that top the list, a number are considered underperformers. The United States, for instance, consistently scores below the average of other OECD countries on the international PISA examination, particularly in math and science.[2] India, the second-most-highlighted country, performed so poorly on the 2009 PISA exam that it backed out of future participation.[3] Assessments of younger children in India's rural areas show that fewer than half in the fifth grade can read and about a quarter can do simple division.[4] Brazil is another underperformer, with PISA results that place 15-year-olds on par with middle-income countries in the region, such as Peru and Colombia, but far below the OECD average and middle-income countries, such as Indonesia, Thailand, and Vietnam.[5] Similarly, South Africa performs poorly on international assessments; only 50 to 60 percent of primary students meet basic reading and math proficiency.[6] However, high-performers top the list as well. Kenya's per capita income level is about a quarter of South Africa's, yet nearly all primary school children are proficient in literacy and numeracy.[7] Finland, sixth in our catalog, has embarked on a countrywide effort to identify and promote innovation while consistently topping international rankings. Kenya and Finland also show levels of equity in learning outcomes that are significantly higher than those in the United States, South Africa, Brazil, and India. Education's role in addressing social inequality is an important part of this picture.

### *Focus on Marginalized Communities*

Education innovations often focus on the poorest children (figure 6-4). A majority of innovations, 57 percent, target marginalized populations, including low-income children, out-of-school children, orphans, girls, students with disabilities, ethnic minorities, child laborers, and children in crisis. Forty-seven percent of innovations explicitly target low-income learners. Interestingly, the next greatest share of innovations in the catalog, at 33 percent, has no target population at all; these innovations are more often technology products intended for general consumption, though a smaller piece of this category includes schools that do not seek to serve a specific type of learner. A significant portion of innovations target learners based on geography, such as those meant for children in rural zones, which account for one fifth of the catalog. Despite the heartening trend of focusing on marginalized learner populations, however, the overwhelming majority of learners served by cataloged innovations are already in school. With only 10 percent of innovations targeting out-of-school learners, there is a real need to figure out how to use innovations reach the most marginalized.

Regardless of their individual effectiveness, the innovations collectively point to their potential relevance in a wide range of contexts, including for those that are farthest behind.

### *Leveraging the Expertise of Nonprofits and the Business Community*

A mix of education actors implement our cataloged innovations. As figure 6-5 shows, the smallest share of the innovations, 12 percent, are the result of government policy or initiatives and implemented by ministries of education, including government schools. For-profit companies, largely those in the education technology (or edtech) space, lead the next largest share of innovations, at 26 percent. However, nonprofits in civil society are by far the most common type of actor, implementing more than 60 percent of the innovations in the catalog.

We further classified these innovations according to where they were used—inside of schools, outside of schools, or both inside and outside of schools. In-school innovations include classroom-based learning manage-

**FIGURE 6-4** Majority of Education Innovations
Focus on Marginalized Students

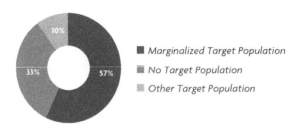

■ Marginalized Target Population

■ No Target Population

■ Other Target Population

ment software, school-based extracurricular programming, and schools themselves. Out-of-school innovations might include programming in a community center or educational games used in the home. According to this classification, over two-thirds of innovations are used inside of schools, whereas less than half are used outside of schools.

## *Mixed Sources of Financing*

On the financing end of innovation, government and nongovernment actors fund a similar share of innovations. No one sector outshines the others; instead, they support innovations at broadly similar levels. For example, even though philanthropic foundations finance the largest proportion of innovations (29%), user fees (27%), government monies (26%), for-profit investments (23%), and community or individual donations (20%) all finance roughly comparable shares. One type of funding that stands out for how little it contributes to supporting education innovations in the catalog is international aid dollars, which support only 11 percent of our catalog. These financing sources support a variety of innovations, from funding schools to after-school music enrichment to in-school robotics labs. The exception is user fees, largely charged by technology-enabled programs delivered by for-profit companies. In fact, more than half of innovations that charge fees are software products such as mathematics applications or course management platforms. Few of these fee-charging innovations are private schools.

**FIGURE 6-5**  Types of Organizations Delivering Innovations

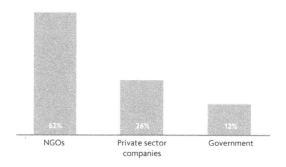

| NGOs | Private sector companies | Government |
| 62% | 26% | 12% |

## *Public-Private Partnerships Used by Many*

Roughly one-fifth of the innovations in the catalog involve some type of public-private partnership (PPP). Broadly defined, PPPs are collaborations between government and nongovernment actors to finance and provide education services. In our catalog, these are almost exclusively nongovernment programs that engage with government actors for little more than funding. More specifically, 78 percent of the 554 cataloged PPPs are financed by governments and are delivered by nonprofits (figure 6-6). These include many charter schools and online teacher support tools.

A much smaller share of these PPPs are privately financed government programs (17%). A further 15 percent of the innovations are delivered by for-profits and use PPPs. Half of the for-profit PPPs involve direct collaboration between government schools and private companies; these generally focus on vocational education and involve government partnering with companies to provide employment and linkage opportunities in specific industries. The other half of these for-profit PPPs use government funding with little public sector involvement in the intervention's day-to-day operations. This model is most common in the United States, where various federal agencies provide funding support to companies developing education technology products through the Small Business Innovation Research program.

**FIGURE 6-6**  Types of Organizations Delivering
Innovations through PPPs

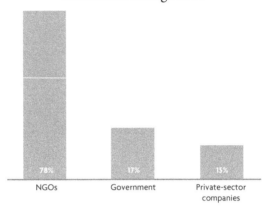

## The State of the Innovation Spotting Community

This cataloging exercise revealed much about Innovation Spotters' priorities—as well as their blind spots. Chief among these findings is that these innovation-spotting efforts largely do not overlap. All told, 11 of the 16 cataloged lists collaborated in some capacity with at least one of the others. Yet only 207 innovations—just under 10 percent of the entire catalog—appear on more than one list. Only a handful of innovations appear on more than three of the lists, including well-known favorites such as Read India; Escuela Nueva; Educate! Experience; and Can't Wait to Learn. These innovations are some of the most well-studied interventions in our catalog. Mostly, however, each Innovation Spotter seems to capture a distinct piece of the education innovation community.

Our catalog's misses, however, are as important as its highlights. Conspicuously absent from the surveyed innovations are efforts targeting displaced children and youth, and those affected by armed conflict or natural disaster. Fewer than 4 percent of innovations, only 119, explicitly target conflict-affected or displaced young people. A survey of innovations' geographies reveals similar concerns: 21 of the 35 countries on the World Bank's Fragile Situations list appear fewer than five times in our catalog, and seven do not appear at all.[8] The sole cataloged list focusing on education in emergencies, the Humanitarian Education Accelerator, highlights just eight innovations at the time of our study.

Undoubtedly, there are many education innovations in these contexts. The Inter-Agency Network for Education in Emergencies (INEE) Minimum Standards for Education: Preparedness, Response, Recovery, and the INEE Toolkit were recently recognized as one of 12 "Innovative Policies 2016" at the UN office in Vienna.[9] The INEE, in fact, has created a resource list that includes more than 1,000 interventions, tools, and resources, many of which could be innovative and informative. One possible reason that Innovation Spotters have not picked up innovations in these contexts might be language and operating frameworks. In contexts of upheaval and instability such as communities affected by forced migration, humanitarian emergencies, or protracted conflict, the idea of innovation may have less relevance as the majority of interventions are likely to be operating outside the traditional education norms formed during more stable times. For example, INEE does not describe the list of interventions and approaches in its toolkit as a collection of innovations, but rather frames the work as an effort to inform and empower governments and humanitarian workers providing education in emergency contexts.[10] For that matter, actors specialized in education in emergencies may rarely interface with the organizations working on broader education reform efforts and may miss cross-fertilization opportunities. Regardless of the reasons, Innovation Spotters are not seeking out innovations for communities affected by displacement, conflict, or disaster. At a time when the world is facing the largest refugee crisis since World War II, the Innovation Spotters seem to be focused elsewhere.

Interventions in the catalog also rarely focus on learners with disabilities. Fewer than 7 percent of interventions are intended for this population, a notable omission considering both technology's potential to level the playing field in learning and the relative prevalence of technology-based interventions in our catalog.[11] Yet we rarely see innovations that leverage the power of technology to improve disabled learners' experiences. Only 75 of the 1,363 innovations that use technology to augment, modify, or redefine practices target children with disabilities.

Innovations developed and implemented by governments also seem to play a modest role in the lists of the Innovation Spotters. Only 12 percent of the innovations in the catalog are implemented by governments, even though one of the Innovation Spotters, the OECD, was dedicated to capturing innovations in government education systems. This omission likely underrepresents the ways that governments attempt to innovate in education. Similar to our hypothesis about children and youth in conflict, governments may be less likely to use the language of innovation to describe their interventions, or may be innovating in ways that the Innovation Spotters may not notice. For example, the Japanese peer-learning model for teachers, Lesson Study, did not make it on to any Spotter list. The model encourages teachers to share knowledge and skills with their peers as they collaboratively plan, observe, and critique each other's lessons each month. The absence of Lesson Study from Spotters' lists is surprising, given the extent to which it has spread across the world and the robustness of its effectiveness evidence. A case study on implementation by the Zambian government, for example, demonstrated that students learning from Lesson Study teachers passed national science examinations at a rate 12.4 percent higher than their peers. Spotters' sights, it seems, are not set on government-led innovations.

## The Potential to Leapfrog: Bright Spots and Gaps along the Leapfrog Pathway

As we cataloged and analyzed these policies, programs, schools, and tools, we reflected on the state of the global innovations community. What innovations are transforming teaching, learning, and recognition, and are they reaching poor children? How do innovations use people, places, technology, and data? Or are the Innovation Spotters focused elsewhere, not illuminating the critical dimensions needed to make the ultimate leap forward and solve the twin problems of skills inequality and uncertainty? We hope that our analysis can contribute to the education innovation community's ability to help leapfrog education.

## *Charting the Bright Spots*

Our analysis uncovered a number of bright spots in the global education innovation community, with activities that are helping to leapfrog education. Chief among these is an overwhelming focus on improving student learning, particularly through playful pedagogies. Nearly three-quarters of all innovations use pedagogical approaches that involve playful learning (figure 6-7).

**Pedagogical Focus on Playful Learning**    In one example, the Indian company FunDa Labz sells building kits that teach math and science concepts through playful creation. Instead of learning about the human ear from a textbook, students might use a FunDa Labz activity kit to build and test a working model of an ear. Other innovations are individual schools identified for their hands-on and experiential practices, including Maria de Socorro Rocha de Castro in Brazil. This municipal primary school is based on a "contextualized learning" model, in which students identify local phenomena that they want to study and collaborate with teachers to develop multidisciplinary learning plans. Students might, for example, discuss the cultivation of a local plant, measure and calculate its average height, research and write about its history, and design an irrigation system to increase production. Still other innovations offer students interactive, real-life learning opportunities where they can explore and experiment with how to solve problems. One such example is the nonprofit JASON, which provides a supplemental science curriculum that targets middle-school science lessons. Learners who have access to a computer and a strong internet connection go on science "missions," working with practicing scientists on projects and doing tasks where they must apply

**FIGURE 6-7**   Innovations That Involve Playful Learning Approaches

69% of innovations use playful learning approaches

their science knowledge to help solve a real-life problem, such as hurricane path prediction.

Notably, innovations aiming to improve learners' vocational skills use student-driven, experiential, iterative, and hands-on approaches more frequently than those that target academic skills. This may not be surprising, as vocational education has always had project-based learning at its heart. One example of such an approach is Guatemala's Ak' Tenamit Internship Program. This NGO-led secondary education program for rural, indigenous Mayan youth splits participants' time between the classroom and a series of internships, where learners apply the concepts learned in class. Unlike other technical schools in the country, where students have an average of between 200 and 250 hours of work experience, young people in Ak' Tenamit spend 3,000 hours working with numerous employers, a strategy that not only hones their skills but also helps them find the area in which they most want to work.

Given the heavy reliance on playful learning approaches, a major focus of innovations in the catalog is to improve 21st-century skills—like critical thinking, confidence, and global awareness—and academic skills—like literacy, numeracy, and science (figures 6-8 and 6-9). A smaller number focus on improving vocational skills, including business skills or those associated with specific trades. Half of all innovations in the catalog aim to improve both academic and 21st-century skills—a promising sign in the movement to develop breadth of skills for all learners. Such innovations focus on helping students to not only remember information, but also to understand it and use it to evaluate information and create new knowledge.

**A Reduced Burden on Teachers**   Another bright spot is the promising trend of unburdening teachers. Almost 40 percent of cataloged innovations employ creative strategies to free up teachers' time and support them in their daily work. CUE's work on scaling up improvements in learning has identified unburdening and empowering teachers as one of the core ingredients for enabling effective interventions to spread. Given the wide range of tasks that teachers must do, including many that have little to do with teaching itself, there certainly is scope for helping better support teachers in their work.[12]

**FIGURE 6-8**   Skill Types Targeted by Innovations

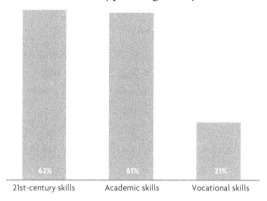

**FIGURE 6-9**   Specific Skills Targeted by Innovations

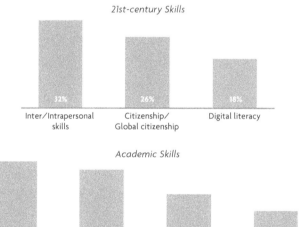

*Including social studies, foreign languages, etc.

One tool to unburden teachers is reaching out to new people and places to help transform students' learning experiences. Teachers are actively incorporating community members, from employers to artists, into their classrooms as content specialists, aides, or other sources of support.

Through the Educurious Expert Network, for example, teachers can set up virtual lessons with experts working in fields related to students' projects and interests. Likewise, the global Getting Ready for School Program trains older children to help younger learners successfully transition to primary school in areas where a formal preschool is not available. A teacher trains these older students, who then use planned playful activities to develop children's school readiness skills.

A more common approach, however, is using technology to remove the burden of administrative tasks. In fact, more than 80 percent of innovations that seek to unburden teachers make use of technology. These include interventions such as classroom management tools, online lesson repositories, and even adaptive games. For example, LDC Core Tools, developed by an American nonprofit, offers frameworks and templates for lesson planning and assessing in line with Common Core State Standards. In Chile, the nonprofit eMat offers online interactive mathematics games and activities aligned with national curriculum standards. Teachers assign learning units to individual students and track performance using an online dashboard.

One of the most common types of unburdening tools featured in our catalog is the learning management system. These software tools support teachers in delivering and tracking lessons, and often facilitate communication among teachers, students, and parents. One such example is Fuel Education, which enables teachers to curate online curricula from an open-source resource library. Teachers can then assign customized lessons to individual learners and receive real-time analytics on student learning. Most of the cataloged learning management systems are in use in developed nations, particularly the United States. This mirrors a broader trend in unburdening teachers: the vast majority of unburdening innovations are used in developed countries, and nearly half are used in the United States.

### Highlighting the Gaps

Nonetheless, several gaps limit the potential of the education innovations community to help leapfrog progress. These gaps reflect a lower level of collective focus on four areas important for leapfrogging: recognizing student learning; developing teachers' skills; leveraging transformative technologies; and regularly and transparently collecting and using data to drive learning and inform programming.

**Recognition of Student Learning**  First, exceedingly few innovations focus on transforming the flip side of the teaching and learning process: how learning is recognized. Despite their focus on playful pedagogies, innovations rarely experiment with individualized learning progressions or hybrid schemes for verifying learners' skills and abilities. Only 15 percent have moved toward more individualized and flexible methods of progressing learners along their educational careers. These innovations generally rely on technology to provide real-time feedback and adapt content to learners' needs. Some of these innovations are supplemental digital curricula delivered by for-profit companies, such as Reading Plus. This reading intervention offers flexible assessments and adaptive instruction that adjust to a student's reading level and interest. Others are learning applications based on mobile phones or tablet computers that create flexibility through gamification. For example, BuzzMath allows learners to create an avatar and progress through various math concepts as they complete competency-based "missions."

An extremely small share of innovations—2 percent—complement education-led credentialing with skills verification by employers or postsecondary institutions. Unsurprisingly, these interventions focus on employability skills, including basic academic knowledge, industry-specific competencies, and interpersonal and intrapersonal skills like collaboration and resilience. For example, Enactus Senegal offers Senegalese university students the opportunity to collaboratively design and lead community development projects. Student teams have developed products like solar ovens and designed management handbooks for farm cooperatives. As students initiate their projects, they participate in life-skills workshops and receive feedback and career guidance from industry professionals. To combat youth unemployment, Enactus Senegal works with corporations and local businesses, which closely monitor student projects and the skills they develop, and even offer job interviews to promising candidates.

However, few interventions transforming verification actually provide education within the formal system. Instead, they are often for-profit programs that collaborate with employers, largely in the technology space, to train learners of any age. A prime example of this model is CodeFights—an online coding game that allows any user to complete challenges based on particular programming concepts. As the user wins challenges of increasing difficulty, he or she is invited to apply to top technology companies that are looking for coders with those specific skills. This arrangement, however, poses the question of how far innovations in teaching and learning can go without the requisite shifts in how students' learning is recognized. Because our catalog relies entirely on publicly available program documents and descriptions, it is possible that some innovative models are working to change how learning is recognized but simply choose not to highlight this piece of their efforts.

The lack of attention to the recognition element of our pathway ultimately proves troubling for a global leapfrog effort. How learning is recognized exerts powerful incentives on the learning experience and shapes how students' progress through education as well as what types of educational experiences students and their parents seek out. Given the strong focus of innovations on transforming the teaching and learning process and their comparatively limited focus on transforming the recognition of learning, the education innovations community may be missing a vital opportunity. Ramping up new approaches to recognizing learning, in line with the leapfrog pathway, could help support the changes aspired to by innovators working to transform teaching and learning.

Teacher Professional Development    Despite the multitude of approaches to unburdening teachers, a surprisingly small percentage of innovations explicitly support teachers' professional development. In making this claim, we considered any innovation whose program language states that it provides professional development opportunities or otherwise seeks to improve teachers' skills. As previously noted, only 23 percent of innovations focus on teacher development. One such effort is the Fabretto Children's Foundation's Early Education Program from Nicaragua, which trains public preschool teachers to use play-based pedagogies. The foundation also shows teachers on how to use locally available supplies to develop their own creative teaching resources. Another is the Rwandan Teacher Training Colleges, which offer online training courses for secondary school teachers. Training modules focus on preparing educators to integrate new teaching practices and technologies into their classrooms.

Support for teachers' capacity to shift how they teach will be central to any successful attempts to leapfrog education. Any serious efforts to add playful learning approaches to classrooms and to foster breadth of skills will require teachers to develop and be comfortable with new strategies and approaches. That less than one-quarter of the innovations in our catalog have an explicit aim of developing teachers' own skills and capacity reflects the limited priority of this crucial piece of the leapfrog puzzle. In-depth discussions involving members of the education innovations community, along with teachers and teacher organizations, could help uncover why there currently is so little focus on teachers' own skill development, as well as what steps could help support teacher professional development in the future.

**Transformative Technology**    Surprisingly, given the rhetoric about technological innovation, few of the innovations cataloged seem to leverage technology and data to help transform education. Just over half of the innovations use technology at all, and most do so in a way that either substitutes or augments existing practice. Only 20 percent of the innovations that use technology aim to do so in a transformative way that redefines and extends what is currently possible in standard education practice. For example, the INQuiry Intelligent Tutoring System relies on real-time assessment and artificial intelligence technology to develop students' inquiry skills. Through its online science learning environment, students complete virtual labs that challenge them to lead the inquiry process from hypothesis generation to communicating their findings. The platform automatically collects data on student progression and inquiry skill development—using algorithms to identify, for example, if a student has designed a controlled experiment. These data are continuously fed into an online teacher portal, which provides classwide and individual performance metrics. Teachers receive real-time mobile alerts on student skills progression, coded by urgency and level of support needed, to allow them to target and assist individual students. An artificial intelligence inquiry coach named Rex the Dinosaur uses these student performance data to provide real-time tutoring, scaffolding student learning as needed if a teacher is not available. Another intervention is iCivics, a nonprofit civic education platform that houses role-playing games and interactive digital tools that place students in the roles of public servants. Likewise, the

Swedish company WriteReader seeks to help young learners improve their literacy skills by creating a platform where they can write and post their own digital books. Readers, usually parents or teachers, can help correct mistakes using the online story hub.

The promise of technology as a transformative educational tool is falling short in the innovations in our catalog. As most of the innovations that do use technology focus on using the tool to either substitute for or augment traditional practice, the education innovations community is not sufficiently leveraging technology to leapfrog education and address skills inequality and skills uncertainty at the same time. Deeper discussions in the technology and education innovations communities could highlight where the barriers are, why they exist, and what can be done to remove or mitigate them.

**Data to Drive Learning and Inform Programming**   Innovation is similarly scarce in the context of data; only 16 percent of cataloged interventions describe how they regularly use data to drive learning and program outcomes. In fact, most innovations share no information about their data practices. The few that use data to transform student learning rely heavily on novel technologies, especially real-time assessment through gamification. One example of this sort of intervention is Dragon Box, an award-winning series of math applications. In role-playing games like Big Numbers and Elements, students learn and practice mathematical concepts while data, collected in real time, are used to determine information presented to learners and how they advance through the story. Another is Sokikom, a collaborative math game that allows learners to progress at their own pace as they demonstrate understanding. Teachers can use an online platform to track students' achievement and assign specific modules to meet learners' needs.

The catalog highlighted a number of innovations working on large-scale data transparency, including the LINK School Performance Review and the Karnataka Learning Partnership. The former is a community-driven process implemented in sub-Saharan Africa that helps district education officials collect data on teaching and learning, school leadership, and other education metrics. It then collaborates with educators and community members to develop data-based school and district improvement plans. The latter is a web-based platform that allows stakeholders in India's

Karnataka state to share information about their public schools to galvanize systems change.

This problem is not just one of data collection; it also includes data sharing. Just over 800 innovations in the catalog—approximately one-third—make evidence on the effectiveness of their innovations publicly available, and only 2 percent share cost-effectiveness measures. The question arises, then, as to why the other two-thirds do not. For this analysis, we used a generous definition of evidence, counting randomized controlled trials, external evaluations, and internally reported data—even qualitative statements on program efficacy. Of the innovations that do publicly present effectiveness data, roughly 70 percent do so based on internal monitoring and evaluation data.

The type of internal monitoring data made public varies widely. Some innovations merely share a summary of the internal measures they track, such as one that states "this program significantly improved students' academic results over the school year." Others, however, share internally collected data on the specific indicators by which they measure program success. In this context, only 30 innovations in the entire catalog provide evidence from randomized controlled trials—perhaps unsurprising, given the large cost associated with such experiments. But even nonexperimental data from outside sources are rare: fewer than 10 percent of cataloged innovations tout effectiveness evidence collected by external actors.

This gap may be an issue of transparency or prioritization, rather than one of program efficacy. Five Innovation Spotters required some level of impact evidence before including an innovation on their lists. These sources—almost one-third of the catalog—are Development Innovation Ventures, Global Innovation Fund, Humanitarian Education Accelerator, the mEducation Alliance, and R4D's Center for Education Innovations. Additionally, 140 innovations appear on Spotter sublists that require evidence of success—the WISE (World Innovation Summit for Education) Awards finalists and winners, as well as the UNICEF Innovations Fund projects. Roughly 34 percent of the catalog comes from Spotters that required impact evidence. But of these innovations that clearly have evidence of impact, fewer than 40 percent actually make their data public (figure 6-10).

In total numbers, many innovations in the catalog have effectiveness

**FIGURE 6-10** Few Innovations Make Effectiveness Evidence Publicly Available

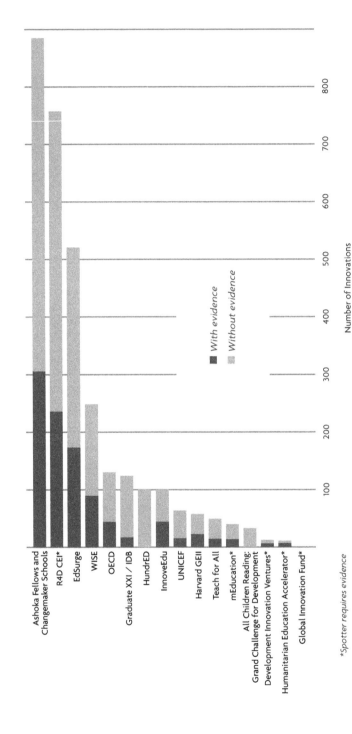

*Spotter requires evidence

data available. However, this reluctance to make public their existing impact data, or to collect effectiveness data at all, is a serious hurdle for the movement to leapfrog education. Educators and students, as well as governments and investors, need a clear idea of an innovation's impact before they consider implementing it themselves.

*Seven*

# Conclusion

The education innovations community is energetic, diverse, and wide-spread. With the innovations profiled in our catalog being practiced in more than 85 percent of the world's countries, there is clearly a move-ment afoot to experiment with the persistent Prussian model of schooling. Children from poor and wealthy families alike are participating in new approaches that are changing, with impressive results, how schooling is delivered, what is taught, and how teaching is done. Ultimately, this rich-ness of education innovations holds promise for leapfrogging education, and for concurrently helping to address the rising trend of income in-equality that is plaguing many societies around the world.

Numerous small- and large-scale innovations have demonstrated that new approaches are both possible and effective, even in low-resource envi-ronments. For example, by providing a hands-on learning experience and an alternative pathway to move young female talent into education, Cam-fed's Learner Guide program is not only building a pipeline of women teachers but also both improving the academic learning outcomes of marginalized girls and boys and helping them develop important social-emotional and leadership skills. Creative approaches to tackling skills in-equality and skills uncertainty are flourishing not only in Tanzania, where the Learner Guide program is in full swing, but also across sub-Saharan Africa and around the globe.

Innovations like Camfed's give hope for the state of the education in-novations community. They demonstrate the ways in which education can transform what and how children learn. The particular leap will depend on the context from which one starts; there are ample examples of innova-tions that help address skills inequality (especially for the most marginal-ized) and, separately, those that help address skills uncertainty. However, what may hold the most promise for education's ability to leapfrog are the innovations that enable marginalized children to simultaneously improve their mastery of school subjects and develop the broader set of skills, such as learning-to-learn and teamwork skills, needed to thrive in an uncertain future.[1]

At their core, the diversity of these innovations demonstrates that new ways of thinking about education are possible and are catching on. After all, mind-sets can stand in the way of leapfrogging as much as any other physical, legal, or financial barriers. In *Schools for 21st-Century Learn-ers*, Andreas Schleicher of the OECD argues that to help children learn, schools need to break free from long-held beliefs about how "things work best."[2] Often, he claims, these deeply held and widely shared beliefs are rooted in past behavior and experiences and are accepted as indisputably correct. Taken together, the leapfrog pathway and the innovations catalog demonstrate a viable set of expanded options that can collectively advance education. These options are not limited by dominant logic or path depen-dence and can exist in poor and rich communities alike.

Nevertheless, leapfrogging will not happen without a concerted focus on scaling up effective approaches. The transformational change needed to address both skills inequality and skills uncertainty cannot take place only with small islands of innovation. To scale up, governments need to be much more engaged in how and when to bring innovative approaches into their ongoing efforts to encourage education system reform and improved management. Governments, as the ultimate duty-bearer of children's right to education, have an important role to play in creating an enabling envi-ronment for new approaches to be tested, and to be shared and scaled if effective. With governments implementing only 12 percent of the inno-vations in our catalog, collaboration across government, civil society, and the private sector will help to scale up innovations with leapfrog potential.

To foster this type of collaboration, the education innovations community must be serious about collecting data. It must be businesslike in evaluating the effectiveness of its approaches and transparent in sharing these data publicly. This effort must include collecting and sharing information on the cost-effectiveness of innovations, as governments rarely can act without such information. It also includes committing to the ongoing use of data during implementation efforts, seeing data as an asset that can help continuously improve innovations and adjust course as needed. This approach to data will support both the effectiveness of the innovation and the ability to understand and articulate to others how it works and under what conditions, pertinent aspects of any conversation about scaling up. Although several innovations given here are serious about collecting data and sharing information publicly, data collection and sharing is not a strong focus in the education innovations community. Good and accessible data are essential for governments and other scaling actors to understand the different types of innovative approaches that could be optimal for leapfrogging—whether in teaching and learning practices or in practices to recognize learning.

Scaling-up activities may include helping governments and other key decisionmakers—such as foreign aid donors, which are the least involved in the education innovations community—understand the vision of leapfrogging, the principles underlying the leapfrog pathway, the ways in which existing innovations could expand existing options for leapfrogging education progress, and the remaining gaps to be filled. A useful first step could be to form a partnership with our Millions Learning efforts to develop what we call "real-time scaling labs" and to document and support the scaling-up process through continuous, collective learning approaches, along with other scaling-up initiatives.[3] Mechanisms and approaches will be needed to connect those innovating in education with those designing and implementing policies in order to effect broad systems change. Likewise, any catalog of leapfrogging innovations with constructive ideas and insights for policymakers will have to sift through information to select what is most relevant, identify ways to adapt approaches to local contexts, and enable timely and open conversations about approaches that can transform children's educational experiences.

Previous Millions Learning research has showed that two of the key ingredients for successful scaling in education are effective use of data and collaboration across government, civil society, and the private sector. Our collective attention and action must be devoted to harnessing the potential of innovations to scale up new ways of tackling skills inequality and skills uncertainty. Leapfrogging in education may hold the best promise for rapidly improving children's chances to develop a breadth of skills and thrive in their future lives.

All concerned citizens must work together to take the next steps that will make leapfrogging a reality. We must push innovators, policymakers, and funders to close the four gaps in practice, and we need to set our sights on bringing promising practices to scale in diverse communities. Above all else, the global community must rally around a leapfrog vision of educational progress. Together, we can create an enabling environment that accelerates progress in education and ensures that we do not leave a generation of young people behind.

# Notes

## Chapter 1

1 Era Dabla-Norris and others, *Causes and Consequences of Income Inequality: A Global Perspective* (Washington, D.C.: International Monetary Fund, 2015), 4, www.imf.org/external/pubs/ft/sdn/2015/sdn1513.pdf.

2 David Baker, "Social Theory and the Coming Schooled Society," in *Education in a New Society* (forthcoming, 2018); and David Baker, *The Schooled Society: The Educational Transformation of Global Culture* (Stanford University Press, 2014).

3 Richard V. Reeves, *Dream Hoarders: How the American Upper Middle Class Is Leaving Everyone Else in the Dust, Why That Is a Problem, and What to Do about It* (Brookings Institution Press, 2017).

4 Rebecca Winthrop, "Indian Pupils Invent Their Own Lessons," BBC News, November 16, 2016.

5 Education Commission [International Commission on Financing Global Education Opportunity], *The Learning Generation: Investing in Education for a Changing World* (New York: International Commission on Financing Global Education Opportunity, 2016), 68, http://report.educationcommission.org/report.

## Chapter 2

1 Yasemin Nuhoglu Soysal and David Strang, "Construction of the First Mass Education Systems in Nineteenth-Century Europe," *Sociology of Education* 62, no. 4 (1989): 277–88, doi:10.2307/2112831.

2 Ellwood P. Cubberley, *Public Education in the United States* (Cambridge, Mass.: Riverside Press, 1947).

3 Cynthia B. Lloyd, Carol E. Kaufman, and Paul Hewett, "The Spread of Primary Schooling in Sub-Saharan Africa: Implications for Fertility Change," *Population and Development Review* 26, no. 3 (2000): 483–515, doi:10.1111/j.1728-4457.2000.00483.x.

4 Baker, *The Schooled Society*.

5 Rebecca Winthrop and Eileen McGivney, *Why Wait 100 Years? Bridging the Gap in Global Education*, Brookings Institution, November 28, 2016, www.brookings.edu/research/why-wait-100-years-bridging-the-gap-in-global-education/.

6 Ibid.

7 Claudia Wallis and Sonja Steptoe, "How to Bring Our Schools out of the 20th Century," *Time*, December 10, 2006.

8 On reading, see D. A. Gamson, X. Lu, and S. A. Eckert, "Challenging the Research Base of the Common Core State Standards: A Historical Reanalysis of Text Complexity," *Educational Researcher* 42, no. 7 (2013): 381–91, doi:10.3102/0013189x13505684. On mathematics, see David Baker, Hilary Knipe, John Collins, Eric Cummings, Juan Leon, Clancy Blair, and David Gamson, "One Hundred Years of Elementary School Mathematics in the United States: A Content Analysis and Cognitive Assessment of Textbooks from 1900 to 2000," *Journal for Research in Mathematics Education* 41, no. 4 (2010): 383–424. See also Jennifer McMurrer, "Choices, Changes, and Challenges: Curriculum and Instruction in the NCLB Era," Center on Education Policy, July 24, 2007, www.cep-dc.org/displayDocument.cfm?DocumentID=312.

9 Larry Cuban, *How Teachers Taught: Constancy and Change in American Classrooms, 1890–1990* (New York: Teachers College Press, 1993).

10 Baker, *The Schooled Society*.

11 Colette Chabbott, *Constructing Education for Development: International Organizations and Education for All* (New York: Routledge, 2009).

12 Julia Resnik, *The Organization of School Knowledge: Official Curricula in Global Perspective* (Rotterdam: Sense Publishers, 2008).

13 J. Hiebert and others, "Highlights from the TIMSS 1999 Video Study of Eighth Grade Mathematics Teaching," U.S. Department of Education, National Center for Education Statistics, 2003.

14 Winthrop and McGivney, *Why Wait 100 Years?*

15 Of "1.4 billion school-aged children, 825 million will not be on track to reach 'low' proficiency on PISA, [and] 420 million will not be on track to meet 'low' proficiency on TIMSS [Trends in International Mathematics and Science Study] and PIRLS [Progress in International Reading Literacy Study] (primary-level skills)." Education Commission, *The Learning Generation*, 30.

16 Education Commission, *The Learning Generation*.

17 UNESCO, *Global Education Monitoring Report: Education for People and Planet: Creating Sustainable Futures for All* (Paris: UNESCO, 2016), http://unesdoc.unesco.org/images/0024/002457/245752e.pdf.

18 UNESCO, "World Inequality Database on Education," UNESCO Global Education Monitoring Report 2016, www.education-inequalities.org/.

19 Richard J. Murnane and Greg J. Duncan, *Whither Opportunity? Rising Inequality, Schools, and Children's Life Chances* (New York: Russell Sage Foundation, 2011), 9.

20 Ibid.

21 OECD, *PISA 2012 Results: Creative Problem Solving—Students' Skills in Tackling Real-Life Problems*, vol. V (Paris: OECD Publishing, 2014), doi:10.1787/9789264208070-en.

22 For more information on measuring nonacademic skills, see Fernando M. Reimers and Connie K. Chung, eds., *Teaching and Learning for the Twenty-First Century: Educational Goals, Policies, and Curricula from Six Nations* (Cambridge, Mass.: Harvard Education Press, 2016); and Koji Miyamoto, Maria del Carmen Huerta, Katarzyna Kubacka, Hiroko Ikesako, and Elodie Isabel de Oliveira, *Skills for Social Progress: The Power of Social and Emotional Skills* (Paris: OECD, 2015), doi:10.1787/9789264226159-en.

23 Winthrop and McGivney, *Why Wait 100 Years?*

24 Education for All Global Monitoring Report, "Teaching and Learning: Achieving Quality for All" (Paris: UNESCO, 2014).

25 Murnane and Duncan, *Whither Opportunity?*

26 Sean F. Reardon and Ximena A. Portilla, "Recent Trends in Income, Racial, and Ethnic School Readiness Gaps at Kindergarten Entry," *AERA Open* 2, no. 3 (2016), 12, doi:10.1177/2332858416657343.

27 UNESCO Institute for Statistics (UIS) and UNESCO, *Global Report on Out-of-School Children, 2015* (Montreal: UIS, 2015), p. 39, www.uis.unesco.org/Education/Documents/oosci-global-report-en.pdf: "In countries in the final mile, it is clear that there is an urgent need for specially-targeted efforts to overcome the particular barriers that keep the hardest-to-reach children out of school. They will not be reached simply by business-as-usual approaches that expand existing education systems still further. Instead, there needs to be a shift towards greater equity in education, moving away from systems that allocate resources uniformly and towards systems that allocate resources according to actual needs of marginalised children."

28 Hugh D. Hindman, *The World of Child Labor: An Historical and Regional Survey* (Armonk, N.Y.: M. E. Sharpe, 2009), 4; and UNESCO Institute for Statistics (UIS) and UNICEF, *Fixing the Broken Promise of Education for All: Findings from the Global Initiative on Out-of-School Children* (Montreal: UIS, 2015), doi:10.15220/978-92-9189-161-0-en.

29 Raja Bentaouet Kattan and Nicholas Burnett, *User Fees in Primary Education* (Washington, D.C.: World Bank, 2004).

30 UIS and UNICEF, *Fixing the Broken Promise of Education for All.* For a thorough analysis of out-of-school children and the barriers they face, see also Pauline Margaret Rose, Ricardo Sabates, Benjamin Matthew Alcott, and Ioana Sonia Ilie, "Overcoming Inequalities Within Countries to Achieve Global Convergence in Learning," Background Paper for Education Commission, Research for Equitable Access and Learning (REAL) Centre (Cambridge, UK: University of Cambridge, 2017).

31 Lant Pritchett, *The Rebirth of Education: Schooling Ain't Learning* (Washington, D.C.: Center for Global Development, 2013), 14.

32 One in four primary-school-aged children are not in school, and the other three-fourths of children not learning are in school. Education Commission, *The Learning Generation*, 33.

33 Halsey Rogers, "The 'Nini' Youth of Latin America: Out of School, Out of Work, and Misunderstood," World Bank, January 25, 2016, http:// blogs.worldbank.org/education/nini-youth-latin-america-out-school-out-work-and-misunderstood; and Raja Bentaouet Kattan and Miguel Székely, "Analyzing the Dynamics of School Dropout in Upper Secondary Education in Latin America: A Cohort Approach," Policy Research Working Paper 7223 (Washington, D.C.: World Bank, 2015).

34 UNESCO Institute for Statistics, "A Teacher for Every Child: Projecting Global Teacher Needs from 2015 to 2030," UIS Fact Sheet no. 27 (Montreal: UIS, 2013).

35 Jane Benbow, Adela Mizrachi, Dan Oliver, and Laisha Said-Moshiro, "Large Class Sizes in the Developing World: What Do We Know and What Can We Do?" American Institutes for Research under the EQIP1 LWA, 2007, http:// pdf.usaid.gov/pdf_docs/Pnadk328.pdf; and Results for Development Institute (R4D), *Global Book Fund Feasibility Study: Final Report* (Washington, D.C.: R4D, 2016), http://pdf.usaid.gov/pdf_docs/PA00M8BK.pdf.

36 Education Commission, *The Learning Generation*, 66.

37 Tessa Bold, Deon Filmer, Gayle Martin, Ezequiel Molina, Christophe Rockmore, Brian Stacy, Jakob Svensson, and others, "What Do Teachers Know and Do? Evidence from Primary Schools in Africa," World Bank Policy Research Working Paper 7956 (Washington, D.C.: World Bank, 2017).

38 Global Education Monitoring Report, "If You Don't Understand, How Can You Learn?," Policy Paper 24 (Paris: UNESCO, February 2016); Education Commission, *The Learning Generation*, 62; and Carol Benson, "School Access for Children from Non-Dominant Ethnic and Linguistic Communities," paper commissioned for UIS and UNICEF, *Fixing the Broken Promise of Education for All*, 2014.

39 "Remedial Education," Abdul Latif Jameel Poverty Action Lab, www. povertyactionlab.org/scale-ups/remedial-education.

40 Education Commission, *The Learning Generation*, 93–94.

41 Winnie V. Mitullah, Romaric Samson, Pauline M. Wambua, and Samuel

Balongo, "Building on Progress: Infrastructure Developments Still a Major Challenge in Africa," Afrobarometer Round 6, Dispatch No. 69, 2016.

42 Erik Brynjolfsson and Andrew McAfee, *The Second Machine Age: Work, Progress, and Prosperity in a Time of Brilliant Technologies* (New York: W. W. Norton, 2016).

43 Thomas Friedman, *Thank You for Being Late: An Optimist's Guide to Thriving in the Age of Accelerations* (New York: Farrar, Straus and Giroux, 2016).

44 Claudia Goldin and Lawrence Katz, *The Race between Education and Technology: The Evolution of U.S. Educational Wage Differentials, 1890 to 2005* (Cambridge, Mass.: Harvard University Press, 2008).

45 Hasan Bakhshi, Jonathan Downing, Michael Osborne, and Philippe Schneider, *The Future of Skills: Employment in 2030* (London: Pearson and Nesta, 2017).

46 David H. Autor, Frank Levy, and Richard J. Murnane, "The Skill Context of Recent Technological Change: An Empirical Exploration," *Quarterly Journal of Economics* 118, no. 4 (2003): 1279–333.

47 See, for example, McKinsey Global Institute, "Jobs Lost, Jobs Gained: Workforce Transitions in a Time of Automation," McKinsey & Company, 2017; World Economic Forum, *The Future of Jobs: Employment, Skills and Workforce Strategy for the Fourth Industrial Revolution* (Geneva: World Economic Forum, 2016), http://www3.weforum.org/docs/WEF_FOJ_Executive_Summary_Jobs .pdf; and OECD, *Getting Skills Right: Skills for Jobs Indicators* (Paris: OECD Publishing, 2017).

48 See, for example, Daron Acemoglu and David Autor, "Skills, Tasks and Technologies: Implications for Employment and Earnings," in *Handbook of Labor Economics*, vol. 4, Part B, edited by David Card and Orley Ashenfelter (New York: Elsevier, 2011): 1043–171.

49 Bakhshi, Downing, Osborne, and Schneider, *The Future of Skills*.

50 See, for example, Peter Mueser, "The Effects of Noncognitive Traits," in *Who Gets Ahead? Determinants of Economic Success in America*, edited by Christopher Jencks and others (New York: Basic Books, 1979): 122–58.

51 James J. Heckman, "Lessons from the Bell Curve," *Journal of Political Economy* 103, no. 5 (1995): 1091–120.

52 See, for example, James J. Heckman, Jora Stixrud, and Sergio Urzua, "The Effects of Cognitive and Noncognitive Abilities on Labor Market Outcomes and Social Behavior," *Journal of Labor Economics* 24, no. 3 (2006): 411–82; World Economic Forum, *The Future of Jobs* (2016); and Goldin and Katz, *The Race between Education and Technology*.

53 Bakhshi, Downing, Osborne, and Schneider, *The Future of Skills*.

54 Mark Muro, Sifan Liu, Jacob Whiton, and Siddharth Kulkarni, *Digitalization and the American Workforce* (Washington, D.C.: Brookings Institution, 2017), www.brookings.edu/wp-content/uploads/2017/11/mpp_2017nov15_digitali zation_full_report.pdf.

55 David H. Autor, "The 'Task Approach' to Labor Markets: An Overview," NBER Working Papers no. 18711 (Cambridge, Mass.: National Bureau of Economic Research, 2013).

56 Melanie Arntz, Terry Gregory, and Ulrich Zierahn, "The Risk of Automation for Jobs in OECD Countries: A Comparative Analysis," OECD Social, Employment and Migration Working Papers, No. 189 (Paris: OECD Publishing, 2016), doi:10.1787/5jlz9h56dvq7-en.

57 Ibid.

58 World Economic Forum, *The Future of Jobs* (2016).

59 World Economic Forum, *The Future of Jobs and Skills in Africa* (Geneva: World Economic Forum, May 2017), http://www3.weforum.org/docs/WEF_EGW_FOJ_Africa.pdf.

60 Education Commission, *The Learning Generation*.

61 World Economic Forum, *The Future of Jobs* (2016).

62 Maria E. Canon, and Elise Marifian, "Job Polarization Leaves Middle-Skilled Workers out in the Cold," Federal Reserve Bank of St. Louis, January 2013, www.stlouisfed.org/publications/regional-economist/january-2013/job-polarization-leaves-middleskilled-workers-out-in-the-cold; and Indhira Santos, "Labor Market Polarization in Developing Countries: Challenges Ahead," World Bank, June 14, 2016, http://blogs.worldbank.org/developmenttalk/labor-market-polarization-developing-countries-challenges-ahead.

63 Richard Dobbs, Anu Madgavkar, Dominic Barton, Eric Labaye, James Manyika, Charles Roxburgh, Susan Lund, and others, *The World at Work: Jobs, Pay, and Skills for 3.5 Billion People* (Washington, D.C.: McKinsey & Company, 2012), www.mckinsey.com/global-themes/employment-and-growth/the-world-at-work.

64 Julie Coiro, Michele Knobel, Colin Lankshear, and Donald J. Leu, eds., *Handbook of Research on New Literacies* (New York: Routledge, 2014).

65 Rebecca Winthrop and Eileen McGivney, "Skills for a Changing World: Advancing Quality Learning for Vibrant Societies," Brookings Institution, 2016, www.brookings.edu/wp-content/uploads/2016/05/global_20160809_skills_for_a_changing_world.pdf.

66 Reimers and Chung, *Teaching and Learning for the Twenty-First Century*.

67 Yong Zhao, *World Class Learners: Educating Creative and Entrepreneurial Students* (Thousand Oaks, Calif.: Corwin, 2012).

68 Naveen Menon, Joel Nicholson, and Fouad Roukoz, "Rethinking K-12 Education: Defining a New Model," A. T. Kearney, 2014, www.atkearney.com/documents/10192/4540067/Rethinking K-12 Education.pdf/d385bd9b-b3af-4653-b5ea-727d2197ce98.

69 For more information, see Winthrop and McGivney, "Skills for a Changing World."

## Chapter 3

1 See, for example, "About Us," Leap Innovations, n.d., www.leapinnovations. org/about-us; Helen Walters, "Reinventing Education for Millennials: Anant Agarwal at TEDGlobal 2013," TED Blog, June 14, 2013, http://blog.ted.com/ reinventing-education-for-millennials-anant-agarwal-at-tedglobal-2013/; and "FGV Opens Center for Excellence and Innovation in Education Policies," FGV Notícias, November 28, 2016, http://fgvnoticias.fgv.br/en/news/fgv-opens-center-excellence-and-innovation-education-policies#.

2 Marcelo M. Suárez-Orozco and Carolyn Sattin, "Introduction: Learning in the Global Era," in *Learning in the Global Era: International Perspectives on Globalization and Education*, ed. Marcelo M. Suárez-Orozco (Berkeley: University of California Press, 2007), 1.

3 "Life Expectancy," World Health Organization (WHO), n.d., www.who.int/ gho/mortality_burden_disease/life_tables/situation_trends_text/en/.

4 Rebecca Winthrop and Gene Sperling, *What Works in Girls' Education: Evidence for the World's Best Investment* (Brookings Institution Press, 2015), 29.

5 Ibid.

6 World Bank, "World Bank Forecasts Global Poverty to Fall Below 10% for First Time; Major Hurdles Remain in Goal to End Poverty by 2030," World Bank, October 2015, www.worldbank.org/en/news/press-release/2015/10/04/ world-bank-forecasts-global-poverty-to-fall-below-10-for-first-time-major-hurdles-remain-in-goal-to-end-poverty-by-2030.

7 Edwin Dean, *Education and Economic Productivity* (Cambridge, Mass.: Ballinger Publishing, 1984).

8 Robert J. Barro and Jong Wha Lee, "A New Data Set of Educational Attainment in the World, 1950–2010," *Journal of Development Economics* 104 (2013): 184–98.

9 Jeff Howe, *Crowdsourcing: Why the Power of the Crowd Is Driving the Future of Business* (New York: Three Rivers Press, 2009).

10 James Coleman, "Families and Schools," *Educational Researcher* 16, no. 6 (1987): 32–38.

11 Ibid.

12 Benedict Anderson, *Imagined Communities: Reflections on the Origin and Spread of Nationalism* (London: Verso, 2016).

13 Kenneth D. Bush and Diana Saltarelli, *The Two Faces of Education in Ethnic Conflict: Towards a Peacebuilding Education for Children* (Florence: UNICEF, 2001).

14 Walter W. McMahon reviews the literature (and his own quantitative work) on education's impact on a variety of outcomes and finds positive impact on both democracy and human rights, especially from investments in secondary education, along with other public goods. Walter W. McMahon, "The Social and External Benefits of Education," in *International Handbook on the*

*Economics of Education*, edited by Geraint Johnes and Jill Johnes (Cheltenham, UK: Edward Elgar, 2004), 211–59.

15 Gudrun Ostby and Henrik Urdal, "Education and Conflict: What the Evidence Says," PRIO Policy Brief (Oslo: Peace Research Institute Oslo, 2011).

16 Esther Care and Kate Anderson, *How Education Systems Approach Breadth of Skills* (Washington, D.C.: Brookings Institution, 2016), www.brookings.edu/wp-content/uploads/2016/05/brookings_how-education-systems-approach-breadth-of-skills_web_07-2016.pdf.

17 Ministerial Council on Education, Employment, Training and Youth Affairs (MCEETYA), "Melbourne Declaration in Educational Goals for Young Australians" (Carlton South, Australia: MCEETYA, 2008).

18 For example, the Partnership for 21st Century Learning—developed as a collaboration between business, educators, and government—sets out four large domains: life and career skills; learning and innovation skills; information, media, technology skills; and academic subjects and 21st-century themes. For more details, see "Framework for 21st Century Learning," Partnership for 21st Century Learning, n.d., www.p21.org/about-us/p21-framework.

19 Care and Anderson, *How Education Systems Approach Breadth of Skills.*

20 International Commission on Education for the Twenty-First Century, *Learning: The Treasure Within* (Paris: UNESCO, 1996), http://unesdoc.unesco.org/images/0010/001095/109590eo.pdf.

21 Howard Gardner, *Five Minds for the Future* (Boston: Harvard Business Review Press, 2009), 1.

22 Ibid.

23 Personal communication, Shankar Maruwada and Rebecca Winthrop, May 2017, Brookings Institution, Washington, D.C.

24 Global Education Monitoring Report, *Education for People and Planet: Creating Sustainable Futures for All* (Paris: UNESCO, 2016), http://unesdoc.unesco.org/images/0024/002457/245752e.pdf.

25 Melanie Frost and Angela W. Little, "Children's Learning Practices in Ethiopia: Observations from Primary School Classes," *Oxford Review of Education* 40, no. 1 (2014): 91–111, doi.org/10.1080/03054985.2013.873526.

26 Luis Benveniste, Jeffery Marshall, and M. Caridad Araujo, *Teaching in Cambodia* (Washington, D.C.: World Bank, 2008), https://openknowledge.worldbank.org/handle/10986/8073.

27 Frances Vavrus, Matthew Thomas, and Lesley Bartlett, *Ensuring Quality by Attending to Inquiry: Learner-Centered Pedagogy in Sub-Saharan Africa* (Addis Ababa: UNESCO International Institute for Capacity Building in Africa, 2011). See also Bold and others, "What Do Teachers Know and Do?"

28 Alfonso Echazarra, Daniel Salinas, Ildefonso Méndez, Vanessa Denis, and Giannina Rech, "How Teachers Teach and Students Learn: Successful Strategies for School," OECD Education Working Papers No. 130 (Paris: OECD, 2016), doi:10.1787/5jm29kpt0xxx-en.

29  See also Daniel Ansari, Johannes König, Marilyn Leask, and Tracey Tokuhama-Espinosa, "Developmental Cognitive Neuroscience: Implications for Teachers' Pedagogical Knowledge," in *Pedagogical Knowledge and the Changing Nature of the Teaching Profession*, ed. Sonia Guerrero (Paris: OECD, 2017), 197, doi:10.1787/9789264270695-en; Keith Sawyer, "Conclusion: The Future of Learning: Grounding Educational Innovation in the Learning Sciences," in *The Cambridge Handbook of the Learning Sciences*, 2nd ed., ed. Keith Sawyer (Cambridge University Press, 2014), 726–46; Victor Benassi, Elizabeth M. Tappin, Catherine E. Overson, Michael J. Lee, Edward J. O'Brien, Barbara Prudhomme White, Jennifer J. Stiegler-Balfour, and others, "Applying the Science of Learning: The Cognition Toolbox," in *Applying Science of Learning in Education: Infusing Psychological Science into the Curriculum*, ed. Victor Benassi, Catherine E. Overson, and Christopher M. Hakal (Washington, D.C.: Society for the Teaching of Psychology, 2014), 194; and Hiebert and others, "Highlights from the TIMSS 1999 Video Study of Eighth Grade Mathematics Teaching."

30  Sawyer, "Conclusion."

31  Ibid.

32  John Dewey, *Democracy and Education* (New York: Macmillan Company, 1944); and Paulo Freire, *Pedagogy of the Oppressed* (London: Penguin Books, 2017).

33  Charles Leadbeater, *The Problem Solvers: The Teachers, the Students and the Radically Disruptive Nuns Who Are Leading a Global Learning Movement* (London: Pearson, 2016).

34  See, for example, Clayton M. Christensen, Michael B. Horn, and Curtis W. Johnson, *Disrupting Class: How Disruptive Innovation Will Change the Way the World Learns* (New York: McGraw-Hill, 2008); Larry Keeley, *Ten Types of Innovation: The Discipline of Building Breakthroughs* (Hoboken, N.J.: John Wiley & Sons, Inc., 2013); and Sven Voelpel, Marius Leibold, and Eden B. Tekie, "The Wheel of Business Model Reinvention: How to Reshape Your Business Model to Leapfrog Competitors," *Journal of Change Management* 4, no. 3 (2004): 259–76, doi:10.1080/1469701042000212669. In academic literature more broadly, "leapfrogging" as a term is used to describe widely different concepts across diverse disciplines, from patterns of urban development to improvements in hospital performance to descriptions of voting patterns. There is no clear definition that cuts across disciplines. See, for example, "Look Before You Leap," *The Economist*, August 6, 2016; and Simon Sommer, "Commentary: Leapfrogging as a Principle for Research on Children and Youth in Majority World Settings," *Journal of Research on Adolescence* 23, no. 1 (2013): 187–88, doi:10.1111/j.1532-7795.2012.00835.x.

35  Rebecca Winthrop, "How Can We 'Leapfrog' Educational Outcomes?" *Stanford Social Innovation Review*, November 7, 2016, https://ssir.org/articles/entry/how_can_we_leapfrog_educational_outcomes.

36  Ibid.

37  John Moravec and Arthur Hawkins, Leapfrog Initiatives, n.d., http://leapfrog. umn.edu/.

38  John Moravec, *Knowmad Society* (Minneapolis: Education Futures LLC, 2013), 18.

39  Ibid., 21.

### Chapter 4

1  See, for example, the debates within the global education community leading up to the development of the United Nations Sustainable Development Goal 4 on education, including debates taking place within the Learning Metrics Task Force; "Learning Metrics Task Force," Brookings Institution, May 11, 2017, www.brookings.edu/product/learning-metrics-task-force/.

2  "Madagascar," Education in Madagascar | Global Partnership for Education, n.d., www.globalpartnership.org/country/madagascar.

3  Valerie Strauss, "No, Finland Isn't Ditching Traditional School Subjects. Here's What's Really Happening," *Washington Post*, March 26, 2015.

4  Personal communication, Dzingai Mutumbuka and Rebecca Winthrop, September 27, 2012, at Learning Metrics Task Force, New York City.

5  C. K. Prahalad and Richard A. Bettis, "The Dominant Logic: A New Linkage between Diversity and Performance," *Strategic Management Journal* 7, no. 6 (1986): 485–501, doi:10.1002/smj.4250070602.

6  Esther Care, Helyn Kim, Kate Anderson, and Emily Gustafsson-Wright, *Skills for a Changing World: National Perspectives and the Global Movement* (Washington, D.C.: Brookings Institution, 2017), www.brookings.edu/wp-content/uploads/2017/03/global-20170324-skills-for-a-changing-world.pdf.

7  Care, Anderson, and Kim, *Visualizing the Breadth-of-Skills Movement Across Education Systems.*

8  Care, Kim, Anderson, and Gustafsson-Wright, *Skills for a Changing World.*

9  Education Commission, *The Learning Generation.*

10  Ibid., 68.

11  Rebecca Winthrop, Eileen McGivney, Timothy Williams, and Priya Shankar, "Innovation and Technology to Accelerate Progress in Education," Background Paper for Education Commission, Center for Universal Education (CUE) (Washington, D.C.: Brookings Institution, 2016).

### Chapter 5

1  We were inspired in particular by the work from the University of Minnesota's Leapfrog Institute, including that of John Moravec and Arthur Hawkins (http://leapfrog.umn.edu/).

2  We developed this case study through careful review of publicly available online documents, including those found on the NAVE website (www.oifuturo.org. br/en/education/nave/), and personal communications with Rafael Parente, the former undersecretary of education for the city of Rio de Janeiro.

3  David K. Evans and Anna Popova, "What Really Works to Improve Learning in Developing Countries? An Analysis of Divergent Findings in Systematic Reviews," Policy Research Working Paper 7203 (Washington, D.C.: World Bank, 2015).

4  "Hattie Ranking: 252 Influences and Effect Sizes Related to Student Achievement," Visible-Learning.org (December 2017), https://visible-learning .org/hattie-ranking-influences-effect-sizes-learning-achievement.

5  Birte Snilstveit, Jennifer Stevenson, Radhika Menon, Daniel Phillips, Emma Gallagher, Maisie Geleen, Hannah Jobse, and others, "The Impact of Education Programmes on Learning and School Participation in Low and Middle-income Countries," International Initiative for Impact Evaluation, Systematic Review Summary 7 (London: International Initiative for Impact Evaluation, 2016), doi:10.23846/srs007.

6  See, for example, James W. Pellegrino, "Teaching, Learning and Assessing 21st-Century Skills," in Guerrero, *Pedagogical Knowledge and the Changing Nature of the Teaching Profession*, 245; Ansari, König, Leask, and Tokuhama-Espinosa, "Developmental Cognitive Neuroscience," in Guerrero, *Pedagogical Knowledge and the Changing Nature of the Teaching Profession*, 197; and Benassi and others, "Applying the Science of Learning," in Benassi, Overson, and Hakal, *Applying Science of Learning in Education*, 194.

7  Dewey, *Democracy and Education*, 167.

8  Charles Bonwell and James Eison, *Active Learning: Creating Excitement in the Classroom*, ASHE-ERIC Education Reports (Washington, D.C.: ERIC Clearinghouse on Higher Education, 1991), 18–19.

9  Kathy Hirsh-Pasek, Roberta Michnick Golinkoff, Laura E. Berk, and Dorothy G. Singer, *A Mandate for Playful Learning in Preschool: Applying the Scientific Evidence* (Oxford University Press, 2009).

10  David A. Kolb, *Experiential Learning: Experience as the Source of Learning and Development* (Upper Saddle River, N.J.: Pearson Education, 2014).

11  "Five Characteristics of Playful Experiences," LEGO Foundation, n.d., www.legofoundation.com/en-us/who-we-are/learning-through-play/play-characteristics. Note: The LEGO Foundation provides financial support to the Center for Universal Education.

12  Mitchell J. Nathan and R. Keith Sawyer, "Foundations of the Learning Sciences," in Sawyer, *The Cambridge Handbook of the Learning Sciences*, 21–43.

13  Nancy Butler Songer and Yael Kali, "Science Education and the Learning Sciences as Coevolving Species," in Sawyer, *The Cambridge Handbook of the Learning Sciences*, 565–86.

14  See, for example, Joseph S. Krajcik and Namsoo Shin, "Project-Based Learning," and Jingyan Lu, Susan Bridges, and Cindy E. Hmelo-Silver, "Problem-Based Learning," both in Sawyer, *The Cambridge Handbook of the Learning Sciences*, 275–97 and 298–318.

15  Hilton and Pellegrino, *Education for Life and Work*, 175.

16  Richard E. Mayer, "Should There Be a Three-Strikes Rule Against Pure

Discovery Learning? The Case for Guided Methods of Instruction," *American Psychologist* 59, no. 1 (2004): 16, doi:10.1037/0003-066X.59.1.14.

17 See the website www.innovaschools.edu.pe.

18 Benjamin Samuel Bloom, *Taxonomy of Educational Objectives: The Classification of Educational Goals. Handbook 1: Cognitive Domain* (New York: David McKay, 1974); and Lorin W. Anderson, Benjamin Samuel Bloom, and David R. Krathwohl, *A Taxonomy for Learning, Teaching, and Assessing: A Revision of Bloom's Taxonomy of Educational Objectives* (New York: Longman, 2001).

19 Echazarra, Salinas, Méndez, Denis, and Rech, "How Teachers Teach and Students Learn."

20 Peter Smagorinsky and Richard E. Mayer, "Learning to Be Literate," in Sawyer, *The Cambridge Handbook of the Learning Sciences*, 612.

21 Jane Hansen and P. David Pearson, "An Instructional Study: Improving the Inferential Comprehension of Fourth Grade Good and Poor Readers," *Journal of Educational Psychology* 75, no. 6 (1983): 821–29.

22 Margaret L. Hilton and James W. Pellegrino, *Education for Life and Work: Developing Transferable Knowledge and Skills in the 21st Century*, National Research Council (Washington, D.C.: National Academies Press, 2012), 175, doi:10.17226/13398.

23 We developed this case study through careful review of publicly available online documents, including those found on the Go for Gold website (http://goforgold .org.za/), and personal communications with Bridget-Ann Mullins, Go for Gold's national director, who provided participant quotes and program data.

24 Hattie, *Visible Learning*.

25 Hilton and Pellegrino, *Education for Life and Work*, 180.

26 Sawyer, "Conclusion," in Sawyer, *The Cambridge Handbook of the Learning Sciences*, 726–46.

27 Chris Sturgis, *Reaching the Tipping Point: Insights on Advancing Competency Education in New England* (Vienna, Va.: Inacol, 2016).

28 See Betty McDonald, "Self Assessment and Student-Centred Learning," ERIC – Education Resources Information Center, 2012, http://files.eric. ed.gov/fulltext/ED536980.pdf.

29 Sheryl Grant, "Promising Practices of Open Credentials: Five Years of Progress," Mozilla, February 2017, www.academia.edu/31173947/Promising_Prac tices_of_Open_Credentials_Five_Years_of_Progress.

30 We developed this case study through publicly available online documents, including those found on the Literacy4All website (www.literacy4all.org/), and personal communications with Literacy4All director Catalina González Quintero, who provided participant quotes and program data.

31 Jenny Perlman Robinson, Rebecca Winthrop, and Eileen McGivney, *Millions Learning: Scaling Up Quality Education in Developing Countries* (Washington, D.C.: Center for Universal Education at the Brookings Institution, 2016).

32  Education Commission, *The Learning Generation*.

33  Perlman Robinson, Winthrop, and McGivney, *Millions Learning*.

34  Education Commission, *The Learning Generation*.

35  WHO, *Strengthening the Capacity of Community Health Workers to Deliver Care for Sexual, Reproductive, Maternal, Newborn, Child and Adolescent Health* (Geneva: WHO, 2015).

36  OECD, *Innovative Learning Environments* (Paris: OECD, 2013), 23, doi:10. 1787/9789264203488-en.

37  Ibid.

38  U.S. Department of Education, "Reimagining the Role of Technology in Education," Office of Educational Technology, 2017, https://tech.ed.gov/files/2017/01/NETP17.pdf.

39  Tom Schuller and Richard Desjardins, *Understanding the Social Outcomes of Learning* (Paris: OECD, 2007).

40  Jenny Chanfreau, Emily Tanner, Meg Callanan, Karen Laing, Amy Skipp, and Liz Todd, "Out of School Activities during Primary School and KS2 Attainment," Centre for Longitudinal Studies Working Paper 2016/1 (London: University College London, April 2016).

41  See Herbert Marsh and Sabina Kleitman, "Extracurricular School Activities: The Good, the Bad, and the Nonlinear," *Harvard Educational Review* 72, no. 4 (2002): 464–515, doi:10.17763/haer.72.4.051388703v7v7736; and Elizabeth Covay and William Carbonaro, "After the Bell: Participation in Extracurricular Activities, Classroom Behavior, and Academic Achievement," *Sociology of Education* 83, no. 1 (2010): 20–45, doi:10.1177/0038040709356565.

42  Sudhanshu Handa, Heiling Pineda, Yannete Esquivel, Blancadilia Lopez, Nidia Veronica Gurdian, and Ferdinando Regalia, "Non-Formal Basic Education as a Development Priority: Evidence from Nicaragua," *Economics of Education Review* 28, no. 4 (2009): 512–22, doi:10.1016/j.econedurev.2009.01.001.

43  Matt Dunleavy and Chris Dede, "Augmented Reality Teaching and Learning," in *Handbook of Research on Educational Communications and Technology*, 4th ed., edited by J. Michael Spector, M. David Merrill, Jan Elen, and M. J. Bishop (New York: Springer, 2014), 735–45.

44  Kathy Hirsh-Pasek and Roberta Michnick Golinkoff, "Transforming Cities into Learning Landscapes," Education Plus Development blog, November 2, 2016, www.brookings.edu/blog/education-plus-development/2016/11/02/transforming-cities-into-learning-landscapes/.

45  Jennifer S. Vey and Jason Hachadorian, "Cities as Classrooms: The Urban Thinkscape Project," Metropolitan Revolution blog, July 21, 2016, www.brookings.edu/blog/metropolitan-revolution/2016/07/21/cities-as-classrooms-the-urban-thinkscape-project/.

46  Brenna Hassinger-Das, Kathy Hirsh-Pasek, and Roberta Michnick Golinkoff, "Urban Thinkscape: Using the City As an Agent of Change," Education Plus Development blog, January 5, 2017, www.brookings.edu/blog/education-

plus-development/2017/01/05/urban-thinkscape-using-the-city-as-an-agent-of-change/.

47 We developed this case study through careful review of publically available online documents, including those found on the Mindspark website (https://mindspark.in/), and personal communications with Pranav Kothari, the vice president of Educational Initiatives.

48 Ruben Puentedura, "Transformation, Technology, and Education in the State of Maine," Ruben R. Puentedura's blog, November 26, 2006, http://hippasus.com/blog/archives/18.

49 "Ruben Puentedura on Applying the SAMR Model," Common Sense Media, n.d., www.commonsensemedia.org/videos/ruben-puentedura-on-applying-the-samr-model.

50 Michael Trucano, "Knowledge Maps: ICT in Education," Working Paper 31953 (Washington, D.C.: infoDev/World Bank, 2005).

51 Michael Trucano, "Technologies in Education across the Americas: The Promise and the Peril—and Some Potential Ways Forward," World Bank, Technology & Innovation: SABER-ICT Technical Paper Series 12 (Washington, D.C.: World Bank, 2016), 2, https://openknowledge.worldbank.org/handle/10986/26259.

52 Ibid.

53 Linda Darling-Hammond, Molly B. Zielezinski, and Shelley Goldman, *Using Technology to Support at-Risk Students' Learning* (Stanford, Calif.: Stanford Center for Opportunity Policy in Education, 2014), https://edpolicy.stanford.edu/sites/default/files/scope-pub-using-technology-report.pdf.

54 Barry Fishman, Chris Dede, and Barbara Means, "Teaching and Technology: New Tools for New Times," in *Handbook of Research on Teaching*, edited by Drew H. Gitomer and Courtney A. Bell (Washington, D.C.: American Educational Research Association, 2015), 276.

55 Perlman Robinson, Winthrop, and McGivney, *Millions Learning*.

56 See, for example, the discussion on measuring SDG 4 in UNESCO, "The Data Revolution in Education," Information Paper No. 39 (Montreal: UNESCO Institute for Statistics, March 2017).

57 For a discussion of data practices in education, see Joshua New, "Building a Data-driven Education System in the United States," Center for Data Innovation, 2016, www2.datainnovation.org/2016-data-driven-education.pdf; Michael B. Gurstein, "Open Data: Empowering the Empowered or Effective Data Use for Everyone?" *First Monday* 16, no. 2 (2011), doi:10.5210/fm.v16i2.3316; and Gordon Commission, *To Assess, To Teach, To Learn: A Vision for the Future of Assessment* (Princeton, N.J.: Gordon Commission, 2013), www.gordoncommission.org/rsc/pdfs/gordon_commission_technical_report.pdf.

58 Husein Abdul-Hamid, Sarah Mintz, and Namrata Saraogi, "From Compli-

ance to Learning: A System for Harnessing the Power of Data in the State of Maryland," World Bank Studies (Washington, D.C.: World Bank, 2017), doi:10.1596/978-1-4648-1058-9.

59 UNESCO, "The Data Revolution in Education."

60 Miguel Helft, "Google Uses Searches to Track Flu's Spread," *New York Times*, November 11, 2008.

61 UNESCO, "The Data Revolution in Education."

62 Jonathan Fox, Joy Aceron, and Aránzazu Guillán, "Doing Accountability Differently. A Proposal for the Vertical Integration of Civil Society Monitoring and Advocacy," U4 Issue, Paper No.4 (Bergen: U4 Anti-Corruption Resources Center, 2016).

63 Jonathan Fox, "Social Accountability: What Does the Evidence Really Say?" *World Development* 72 (2015): 346–61; and Jonathan Fox, "The Uncertain Relationship between Transparency and Accountability," *Development in Practice* 17, no. 4–5 (2007): 663–71.

64 Evan S. Lieberman, Daniel N. Posner, and Lily L. Tsai, "Does Information Lead to More Active Citizenship? Evidence from an Education Intervention in Rural Kenya," *World Development* 60 (2014): 69–83.

65 See, for example, Sandy Taut, Flavio Cortes, Christian Sebastian, and David Preiss, "Evaluating School and Parent Reports of the National Student Achievement Testing System (SIMCE) in Chile: Access, Comprehension, and Use," *Evaluation and Program Planning* 32, no. 2 (2009): 129–37; UNESCO, "The Data Revolution in Education"; and Gordon Commission, *To Assess, To Teach, To Learn.*

66 Husein Abdul-Hamid, "What Matters Most for Education Management Information Systems: A Framework Paper," Systems Approach for Better Education Results Working Paper Series No. 7 (Washington, D.C.: World Bank, 2014), http://wbgfiles.worldbank.org/documents/hdn/ed/saber/supporting_doc/Background/EMIS/Framework_SABER-EMIS.pdf.

67 "Learn More about OLI," OLI, Carnegie Mellon University, n.d. http://oli.cmu.edu/get-to-know-oli/learn-more-about-oli/.

68 "1 Day in the Life: The Simon Initiative and Carnegie Mellon's Digital Education Revolution," OLI, Carnegie Mellon University, n.d. http://oli.cmu.edu/1-day-in-the-life-the-simon-initiative-and-carnegie-mellons-digital-education-revolution/.

69 Perlman Robinson, Winthrop, and McGivney, *Millions Learning.*

### Chapter 6

1 As classified by the 2011 International Standard Classification of Education, available at www.uis.unesco.org/Education/DOcuments/isced-2011-en.pdf.

2 See, for example, Drew DeSilver, "U.S. Students' Academic Achievement Still Lags That of Their Peers in Many Other Countries," Pew Research Center,

February 15, 2017, www.pewresearch.org/fact-tank/2017/02/15/u-s-students-internationally-math-science/.

3 Geeta Kingdon, "Opinion: Indian Schools Are Failing Their Students," *New York Times*, December 15, 2015.

4 ASER, *Annual Status of Education Report (Rural) 2016* (New Delhi: ASER, January 2017), http://img.asercentre.org/docs/Publications/ASER%20Reports/ASER%202016/aser_2016.pdf.

5 "Brazil Student Performance (PISA 2015)," OECD Education GPS, n.d., http://gpseducation.oecd.org/CountryProfile?primaryCountry=BRA&treshold=10&topic=PI; and Martin Carnoy, Tatiana Khavenson, Leandro Oliveira Costa, Izabel Fonseca, and Luana Marotta, "Is Brazilian Education Improving? A Comparative Foray Using PISA and SAEB Brazil Test Scores," Higher School of Economics Research Paper WP BRP 22/EDU/2014, 2014, doi:10.2139/ssrn.2539027.

6 UNESCO, "World Inequality Database on Education," *UNESCO Global Education Monitoring Report 2016*, www.education-inequalities.org/.

7 Ibid.

8 "Harmonized List of Fragile Situations FY 17," World Bank, May 9, 2016, http://pubdocs.worldbank.org/en/154851467143896227/FY17HLFS-Final-6272016.pdf.

9 "INEE Wins Innovative Policy Award," Inter-Agency Network for Education in Emergencies (INEE), February 19, 2016, www.ineesite.org/en/blog/inee-wins-innovative-policy-award.

10 INEE, *Minimum Standards for Education: Preparedness, Response, Recovery* (New York: INEE, 2010).

11 See, for example, Mohsen Laabidi, Mohamed Jemni, Leila Jemni Ben Ayed, Hejer Ben Brahim, and Amal Ben Jemaa, "Learning Technologies for People with Disabilities," *Journal of King Saud University—Computer and Information Sciences* 26, no. 1 (2014): 29–45; Heather B. Hayes, "How Technology Is Helping Special-Needs Students Excel," *EdTech*, March 28, 2013, https://edtechmagazine.com/k12/article/2013/03/how-technology-helping-special-needs-students-excel; and Meghan Bogardus Cortez, "Accessible Technology Helps Students with Disabilities Pursue STEM Degrees," *EdTech*, March 10, 2017, https://edtechmagazine.com/k12/article/2017/03/accessible-technology-helps-students-disabilities-pursue-stem-degrees.

12 See, for example, the discussions of teacher tasks in Perlman Robinson, Winthrop, and McGivney, *Millions Learning*; and Education Commission, *The Learning Generation*.

### Chapter 7

1 Andreas Schleicher, *Schools for 21st-Century Learners: Strong Leaders, Confident Teachers, Innovative Approaches* (Paris: OECD Publishing, 2015), 62.

2 Ibid.

3 Jenny Perlman Robinson and Molly Curtiss, "Real-Time Scaling, the 2018 World Development Report, and Getting Millions Learning," Education Plus Development blog, October 6, 2017, www.brookings.edu/blog/education-plus-development/2017/10/06/real-time-scaling-the-2018-world-development-report-and-getting-millions-learning/.

# Index

Page numbers followed by b refer to boxes; those followed by f, to figures, and those followed by t, to tables.

CPSIA information can be obtained
at www.ICGtesting.com
Printed in the USA
LVHW090113040219
606152LV00005B/1/P

9 780815 735700